"I Hate School!"

Some Common–Sense Answers For
Educators & Parents
Who Want To Know Why
& What To Do About It.

by Jim Grant

Published by
Modern Learning Press
Rosemont, New Jersey

ISBN 0-935493-04-2
Item #198

To my wife, Lillian, for her belief in my quest to change the plight of overplaced children; without her unfailing support, this book would never be. And to my sons, Nathan and Caleb, for their understanding of my mission and their willingness to share me.

Acknowledgments

"I Hate School!" was my first published book, and of all my publications, it remains the most important and the one closest to my heart. I therefore especially appreciate the fine work done by the editor of this new edition, Robert Low, "the best friend a manuscript ever had" and a good friend of mine, as well.

In addition to my family and Rob, I would also like to thank the following people for their help and support over the years:

Nancy Richard,
Bob Johnson,
Bert Shapiro,
Linda Skladal,
Jay LaRoche,
and
Garry Myers.

The many other people who have helped me along the way are too numerous to mention here. You know who you are, and you have my heartfelt thanks.

Contents

Foreword

When the first edition of *"I Hate School!"* was published in 1986, it was based on my experiences as a teacher, principal and educational consultant, starting in the 1960's. Much has changed since I was a "rookie" teacher, and much has also changed since 1986, but one of the most important and difficult issues facing parents and teachers remains the same — the failure of many schools to accommodate differences in young children's rates of development and readiness to succeed in school.

Long before the book was published, I had learned that "summer children" whose birthdays fell shortly before the traditional "cut-off" dates for kindergarten entrance — making them the youngest children in their grade — were far more likely to have problems in school than the oldest children in the grade.

And, I had learned that because of young children's varying rates of development, other students were "developmentally young," which meant they were developing at a slower but still normal rate compared to many of their chronological peers. These developmentally young children, also known as "late bloomers," often go on to achieve extraordinary accomplishments when provided with the time they need to grow and learn, along with an appropriate education well-suited to their developmental levels.

However, my experience and that of many educators showed that developmentally or chronologically young children who do not receive the extra time and appropriate education they need often encounter serious difficulties right from the start of their school experience. And, because these young children are forming their own identities and expectations about school at this time, their initial school experiences can often lead to low self-esteem, negative attitudes, and self-destructive behavior patterns. These are the children who end up saying "I hate school!" and acting accordingly, which can have serious long-term effects on their lives, their families, and our society as a whole.

Many parents and teachers have told me that *"I Hate School!"* provided the information and insights they needed to help young children achieve school success right from the start, or to find ways to correct the initial placement of a child in a wrong grade or program. As I had hoped, the book helped these adults see the potential of individual children and assist them in achieving it, rather than simply accepting the poor results of an educational mismatch as a permanent condition. And, it helped these people move beyond the prejudices of the past, so they could recognize that not only is there nothing wrong with a child taking one extra year to progress from kindergarten through high school graduation, it may be the best possible solution to what seems an insurmountable problem.

In the eight years since *"I Hate School!"* was first published, new research has confirmed the success of many "readiness" programs designed to help developmentally and chronologically young children. And, recent studies have shown that teachers across America continue to find that large numbers of students are not ready to learn successfully in the grade or program to which they have been assigned. Promising new developments have also occurred, like the growing popularity of multi-age classes, which offer exciting and effective alternatives for many children, including those who are not succeeding within the traditional lock-step grade structure.

This new edition of *"I Hate School!"* includes recent statistical data, as well as the current thinking of many teachers and educational experts, who are increasingly recognizing the vital importance of readiness and time in a successful education. In my current work as executive director of the Society for Developmental Education, America's leading provider of training in the field of developmentally appropriate education, I have had the privilege of working closely with many such people, and they have been generous in sharing their insights with me.

The book also includes feedback from parents like the mother who wrote the letters included in the appendix of this book. She and many other parents continue to learn firsthand how the reliance on chronological cut-off dates can harm children, and how providing children with extra time to grow and learn can lead to dramatic improvements.

During the last few years, budget cutbacks and ideological opposition have led some schools to resist providing children with the extra time they need. Some ideological extremists now want to prohibit any child in America from ever taking extra time to progress from kindergarten through high school graduation. And, these same extremists claim that theirs is the "developmentally correct" approach to education, even though they have not identified a single school system anywhere in America where this approach is in fact pushing every child from kindergarten through high school in exactly thirteen years.

As in so many of today's conflicts over important issues, those who want to prohibit extra time for children have their own "research" supporting their point of view. This book and others explain how key elements of this research have been shown to be seriously flawed, but the data in question still continues to receive publicity and acceptance in some quarters. So, "I Hate School!" has also been updated to help parents and educators overcome the opposition they may encounter in providing the extra-time options needed by children in their care.

While there are many changes in this new edition of "I Hate School!", its basic message remains the same, because children's basic nature remains the same. Today's children are different in some important respects from their predecessors in previous decades, but they continue to develop and learn at different rates, and so need access to options that meet their varying needs. This concept might seem so simple and straightforward that it's hardly worth stating, but the hard realities found in many of today's schools result in the daily denial of this concept for too many American children.

At the same time, many other children across America now have extra-time options available to them, and are obtaining the multitude of benefits these programs can provide. I hope this revised edition of *"I Hate School!"* will succeed in supporting these programs, and lead to the creation of similar programs for those children now being denied access to them.

The choices made in regard to this issue can determine a child's future success and happiness in life. And, because children are unique individuals — not nameless statistics — the decisions involved are very personal, as well as very important. That's one reason this book was written in a personal way and focuses on the experiences of a number of individuals, including myself. Now, it's time for you to consider this information and make your own decisions about it.

CHAPTER 1
Ready To Succeed, Set Up To Fail

"In every task the most important thing is the beginning, and especially when you have to deal with anything young and tender."
— Plato, *The Republic*

"Everyone thought I was stupid."

"The teacher didn't like me."

"From the very beginning, I felt dumb in school. It wasn't until I entered college, after three years in the service, that I came into my own."

"I hate school!"

Every September, millions of young children walk into school for the first time, filled with excitement, fear, and high hopes. Too many of these students will fail — or feel like failures — before completing their first year. To be more accurate, the school system will fail many of its students. Their enthusiasm will soon turn to sadness and anger, and they'll end up hating school.

Over the years, these children have been called a variety of names — "slow learners," "bored learners," "lazy," "educationally handicapped," "unmotivated," "malcontent," "learning disabled." Is it any wonder that these "severely labeled" students learn to dislike school?

Their inability to meet school requirements has been blamed on everything from inadequate school funding to inadequate parent support, from a lack of discipline to a lack of stimulation, from low teacher salaries to low self-esteem. The list goes on and on. And, while many experts waste time and energy debating where to assign the blame — or even whether the problem exists — too many of these children are way over their heads in school and going under.

Yet, most of the children who are failing or just scraping by in school could succeed. The key is to recognize what they are ready to learn and help them proceed, by placing them where they can meet expectations and succeed. That is, placing them in the right grade or program — the one they are ready for. This might be a different grade than the one many of their chronological peers are in, or it might be a multi-age classroom in which several grades are blended together, or it might be a "transition" class which provides an extra year of continuous-progress education between two grades.

The key is to recognize what they are ready to learn...

Nationwide surveys of elementary school teachers in the 1990's continue to find that about 30 percent of the students are not ready for the grade or program in which they are placed. And, despite all the effort and billions of dollars spent on education reform in the last few decades, this statistic is consistent with the findings of researchers in the 1960's and 1970's.

"Frankly, we found it deeply troubling, ominous really that 35% of the nation's children — more than one in three — are not ready for school, according to the teachers. Even more disturbing, when we asked how the readiness of last year's students compared to those who enrolled five years ago, 42 percent of the respondents said the situation is getting worse; only 25 percent said it's better."
- Ernest Boyer, *Ready To Learn*, citing a 1991 survey conducted by The Carnegie Foundation for the Advancement of Teaching.

"Students are not fully prepared to learn at their grade level...55% of teachers report that all, most or at least more than one-quarter of their students are unprepared...It should be noted that lack of preparedness is a problem at all grade levels."
- 1992 Metropolitan Life Survey of the American Teacher

In recent years, efforts have been made to address this problem by reforming the elementary school curriculum and establishing a "readiness" goal — that by the year 2000, all children will start school ready to learn and succeed in school. The plan for reaching this goal, however, requires extensive changes in the nation's health care system, Head Start programs, and public schools, along with massive amounts of spending. Many of these changes and spending increases have not occurred in time to help today's children— if they have occurred at all — so there is every reason to believe that many children will continue to start school in grades or programs for which they are not ready.

The assignment of children to the wrong grade or program, thereby setting them up for failure, has long-term effects and is itself a tradition that has gone on for too long. There is hardly a person alive in the United States who has not had someone in his family scarred by the experience of failure or marginal performance in school. The anonymous statements at the beginning of this chapter were all made by adults who remember too well the misery they experienced as children.

In previous decades and in recent years, parents and teachers have frequently misread the plight of these children. Too many children being failed by their schools have been labeled "not very bright," "not really trying," or "not living up to their potential." Today, these same children may be suspected of having an "Attention Deficit Disorder." In fact, many bright, motivated, high-potential children with a normal attention span struggle in school because they were assigned to a grade or program in which they had little hope of success.

Simply stated, these children are developing at a different (yet normal) rate compared to many of their peers. Through no fault of their own, their bodies, minds, and emotions have not yet reached the stage required for success in a particular grade or program. These "developmentally young" children are also called "late bloomers" — children who can reach their full (and often extraordinary) potential when schools provide extra-time options that meet these children's needs.

In the course of your life, you probably have known children like these. You may even have been such a child yourself. They are just too plentiful to avoid or ignore. And, when the teachers of the 1990's — just like the researchers of the 1960's — continue to find that almost 1 out of every 3 children is being assigned to a grade or program for which they are not ready, we need to examine the causes and solutions.

Every child is a unique individual

Often, school programs fail to take into account vital differences in the chronological ages, developmental stages, gender, "environmental" factors, and individual needs of children. Yet, these differences can and frequently do determine whether a child experiences success or failure in school. A few brief questions and answers should therefore be considered when evaluating a child's educational options.

Has the child started school at the "right" age?

In nearly all states, the primary means of evaluating a child's readiness for school is counting the number of candles on his or her birthday cake at a particular "cut-off" date. The cut-off dates vary widely from state to *The cut-off* state, so that a child who turns 5 in August may have *dates vary* to wait an extra year before starting kindergarten in *widely from* one state, while just across the state line a child who *state to state...* turns 5 in November may be told to start kindergarten in September, even though he will still be only 4-years-old at that time. In most states, these cut-off dates were set in an arbitrary fashion years or even decades ago, and so are totally unrelated to the difficulty and type of curriculum.

Obviously, the simplistic notion of legal entrance age does not ensure that all children entering school are equally ready for the same educational experience. When you are 5-years-old, six months represents close to one-tenth of the total time you have been alive. A tremendous amount of development takes place during this sort of time span. Nevertheless, in any single grade or program at most schools, there are children as much as twelve months younger than their classmates.

Studies done by Dr. James Uphoff and other research-ers have shown that the younger children in a grade are more likely to experience a number of problems, including failing a grade, being diagnosed as "learning disabled," scoring lower on achievement tests, and dropping out of school. And, Dr. Uphoff has found that this pattern continues all the way through high school.

"While the youngest children [in a grade] made up 23% of the total population of my study, they made up 75% of the 'failed one or more year' subgroup. The oldest children in my study, who had been given an extra year at home before starting school, made up nearly 10% of the total group but 0% of the failure group."
- Dr. James Uphoff, Ed.D., *School Readiness & Transition Programs: Real Facts From Real Schools*

Is the child in the right grade or program at the right time?

Children do not all develop at the exact same rate. Each child has an internal time clock which deter-mines personal growth and development in the emo-tional, social, physical, and intellectual spheres. While other factors can also affect a child's development, there is no way to "make" a child develop faster in or-der to meet the expectations or requirements of a par-ticular school system. Yet, many schools treat children as if they are all at the same developmental stage and are continuing to develop at the same rate, even though numerous studies have shown that there is a wide variation among children's stages and rates of de-velopment at any particular time.

For example, among 5-year-old children you will no-tice a very wide range in height, weight, personality, temperament, and level of experience. The same varia-tions exist in the rate at which these children develop and mature. Yet, in many schools each 5-year-old is expected to master the same curriculum as every other

5-year-old, and do it in the exact same time span — 180 days. Even some "experts" who acknowledge children's developmental differences now claim that only one single program is needed at each grade level, because teachers can simply "individualize" the instruction to meet the diverse needs of all the students in a class.

In reality, even when the curriculum is "developmentally appropriate," some children cannot accomplish or learn all that is needed within a typical 180-day time frame, no matter how much the teacher tries to meet individual needs. And, the increasing diversity, large class sizes, and budget limitations found in many schools make effectively "individualizing" the curriculum an impossibility for many teachers. In addition, many kindergarten programs continue to have a high academic skills content that is not in sync with the developmental needs of most 5-year-olds.

...these children are likely to be identified as "slow"...

So, what is going to happen to those children who are developmentally younger than most of their peers? As early as kindergarten, these children, who may actually be intellectually superior, are likely to be identified as "slow" — a label that may follow them throughout their school careers. At the same time, their temporary inability to master the curriculum will lead to negative feelings about themselves and school — attitudes that may remain with them throughout their school careers.

Is the child a boy or a girl?

Anyone who has ever visited a primary classroom has undoubtedly observed that boys usually have a much harder time there than girls do. The reason is that girls generally mature at a faster rate than boys. By the age of 6, girls are — on average — six months ahead of boys in their development. As children grow older, the gap widens. That's why tenth grade girls love to date twelfth grade boys, and why twelfth grade girls love to date college freshman. Most experts believe that males catch up with females in early adulthood, although some people question whether males ever catch up.

Back in kindergarten and early primary programs, the discrepancy in development between boys and girls makes an enormous difference. As pointed out earlier, six months or a year represents a large percentage of the total life span of a 5 or 6-year-old. In addition, as Dr. Anthony Coletta points out in his book, *What's Best For Kids*, young girls tend to have an advantage over young boys in fine-motor skills such as writing and drawing, while young males are typically better at gross-motor skills such as throwing and catching. The fine-motor system is closely related to the development of language and the ability to read, giving many girls an increased ability to read, spell, talk, and listen.

Under these circumstances, guess how a girl and a boy born on the same day will fare in many primary programs. The girl is likely to make good progress in learning to read and write, enjoy school, and develop confidence in her abilities. The boy is likely to have more trouble sitting still and learning to read and write. He is less likely to enjoy school and develop confidence in his ability to learn and do well in school. He may even be suspected of having an Attention Deficit Disorder, when all he really needs is some extra time to develop.

Are there "environmental" factors or circumstances which may be affecting the child's readiness?

In order to learn in school, children need to be able to focus their attention and listen well, tasks which are much more difficult when a child is also experiencing physical or emotional problems. Parents and teachers therefore should consider a wide range of environmental factors which can have a serious impact on a child's school experience.

Physically, children need to start each day with a good breakfast, so that they have sufficient energy and are not distracted by hunger pangs during the day. They should also have had a good night's sleep, so that they are not struggling to stay awake and focus their attention. Children's vision and hearing ability should be checked frequently, especially if they are having problems in school, or are experiencing headaches, earaches, or allergies. Some experiences during a child's pre-school years which may also affect readiness include exposure to drugs or lead, prematurity, low birth weight, poor pre-natal or post-natal nutrition, and serious or extended illnesses.

Emotionally, young children find it easier to learn when they are not coping with the death of someone important to them, relocation to a home, separation from one or both parents, or the birth of a sibling. Other sources of emotional stress that can affect children's readiness to learn include violence in the home or the community, substance abuse by a parent, and various forms of child abuse or neglect.

What are the individual needs of this particular child?

A child's overall emotional disposition — independent of any environmental factors — is also worth considering. Children who are temperamentally difficult or shy are likely to find a new grade or program more challenging and stressful than a confidant, outgoing child who adapts easily to new situations. And, rather than helping shy or difficult children overcome their temperaments, this sort of situation tends to reinforce such children's negative expectations, creating new obstacles that must also be overcome.

In evaluating a child's readiness for a grade or program, parents and teachers need to consider the unique combination of characteristics which make up the "whole" child, rather than focusing just on one aspect of the child. For example, the fact that a child was born in August does not automatically mean that he or she is unready for a kindergarten program, but a shy, left-handed boy who was born in August, then had a serious illness, and recently moved to town is less likely to be ready than an outgoing, right-handed girl who was born the same day and has since had a very healthy childhood living in the same house.

A parent's understanding of a child, combined with an educator's understanding of the program the child will be participating in, are vital criteria for evaluating a child's educational readiness. This deep, firsthand knowledge is far more important than the statistical data used in academic debates about readiness. Not only have some of the statistics been manipulated by researchers trying to prove a point, but what is right for some or even many children may still be wrong for the particular child under discussion. Children are individuals, after all, not statistics.

Children are individuals, after all, not statistics.

Can you make sure a child is ready for a particular grade or program?

Can you make a child grow an extra twelve inches by this time next year? Of course not. Nor can you appreciably speed up the rate at which a child matures emotionally, socially, physically, or intellectually. What you can do is make sure that a child's readiness is evaluated and considered, and then find the option that best meets the child's needs.

Before or when a child enters a primary grade or program, a fairly simple readiness assessment can provide valuable information about the child's stage of development. (More information about readiness assessments can be found in Chapter 5.) This information, combined with parental input and the observations of educators, can then be the basis for a placement decision which matches the child to a program where the curriculum is appropriate for that particular child, thereby giving the child the best possible opportunity to achieve success in school.

Children who are not developmentally ready for a particular grade or program should have the option of participating in a grade or program that is appropriate for them. This is why many schools have a "readiness" program which provides a year of developmentally appropriate education before kindergarten, as well as "transition" classes which provide an extra year of continuous-progress education after kindergarten. In school districts where such programs are not available, parents may want to have their children attend an extra year of preschool, or have them take two years to complete kindergarten. These sorts of options are discussed in more detail in Chapter 6.

What if a child is already in school and having serious trouble with school work?

Chances are that the child, like tens of thousands of others, may be in a grade or program one year ahead of where the child ought to be. You can help a child in this situation by allowing the child to spend more time in a grade or program in a way that leads to school success. If you find this hard to accept, I can certainly understand, considering the efforts being made by some ideological extremists and administrators to discourage parents and teachers from considering this option. By the time you finish reading this book, however, I believe you will agree that spending more time in a grade or program can relieve certain children of a tremendous burden, and allow them to experience school success.

Why is Jim Grant so sure that extra time can make the difference between school success and failure?

I have seen it happen too many times during my decades of experience as a teacher, principal, and educational consultant. And, I have found that my own professional development parallels that of most other educators, who have come to the same conclusions.

When I was a young teacher with a multi-age class filled with a typically diverse group of 10, 11, and 12-year-old students, I knew that something was drastically wrong, but I did not have the background to identify the problem, much less find the solution.

Nothing in my previous training had prepared me for the situation I faced every single day in that classroom. In those days (and even today) few teacher training institutes provided information about developmental readiness. So, like many other educators, I blamed the children, the textbooks, the parents, and my own inadequacy for the fact that the children's needs were not being met.

Fortunately, when I became the principal of that entire school, I had just enough sense to know when I needed the problem-solving skills of an expert. I turned to Nancy Richard, a child development specialist who is the co-author of an excellent book entitled *One Piece of the Puzzle*, and who happened to have taught me when I was in high school. With her help, I began to observe the wide range of developmental levels among the students within the classes. I could then see clearly that many children were not well-matched with the curriculum and were unable to complete it in the fixed amount of time available.

In attempting to correct this situation, I first tried working with teachers to individualize their programs to meet the needs of each child. This helped some children, but there were others who simply were not ready for the demands of the program to which they were assigned. It was only when the school began providing supportive extra-time options that children like these began to experience their rightful success. In other words, rather than insisting that the children become ready for school, the school became ready for the children.

...the school became ready for the children...

This experience pointed me in an educational direction that has changed my career and my life, as well as the lives of many children who attended my school and other schools I have worked with. The simple but profound concept of readiness is the explanation for many students who are struggling and failing in school.

Providing what children need

Most teachers and parents know when something is wrong with a child's educational experience, and most will do anything they can to correct it. If you could place children in school so that they could learn happily and successfully, wouldn't you do it? Of course you would. The needs of the children in your care are your paramount concern, and their future will depend at least in part on what they experience in school.

Today, we know enough about how children develop and learn to give each child the proper start in school — or, if the child is already in school, to place the child in the proper grade or program. We can help each child achieve success in school, so that no child need ever carry the stigma of school failure. I have written this book to share what I know, hoping that it will contribute to our achievement of this goal.

CHAPTER 2
Failure Hurts For A Long Time

"Unready children are trapped in a situation where they are humiliated in front of their friends every day, and survival becomes a matter of escape by daydreaming...clowning...avoiding school...developing psychosomatic illnesses..."
- Barbara Carll and Nancy Richard, *One Piece of the Puzzle*

I still vividly remember my early school years. I bet you remember yours, too — those early childhood experiences are etched into our brains, unless they were so painful they have been blotted out of conscious memory.

In 1948, the school entrance gate was opened and children flooded in. Other than chronological age and a heart beat, there were virtually no entrance or placement criteria. If you were 5, you were ready.

The only exceptions were the physically and mentally handicapped, who had no federally legislated programs to protect them back then. Once these sorts of children were identified as "rejects," they were sent back home, or in some cases allowed to "pass time" in school until they were old enough to drop out.

The remaining children were divided up into three basic "tracks:"

The low achievers experienced firsthand what it's like to live at the bottom of a caste system. They ended up in the "Buzzard" reading group or class, from which came most of the future dropouts, kids with behavior problems, and users of remedial services. In too many cases, this happened just because the children were developmentally young for their grade or program placement.

The average achievers were designated "Bluebirds," identified by their average scores on a reading readiness test. Though some were intellectually superior but developmentally young, the "average" label clung to them like a burr throughout their school careers.

The teacher's delight were the top scorers on the reading readiness test, children proudly assigned to the "Peacock" reading group. Academic learning came easily for them, but some paid a price in terms of their social and emotional growth.

A few fluent readers — the "gifted and talented" — were moved onto the fast track. Subject to the perils of acceleration, many of these children who skipped over a grade had an important developmental cycle excised from their lives. Usually, they made it up later — by coasting through high school, dropping out of college, or taking a year off in some other way.

More than intelligence goes to school

Back then, educators acted as though children developed only in a single dimension — the intellect. Academic growth was all-important; the emotional, social, and physical aspects of development were ignored.

The tracking of young children in this way failed to take into account the damage that the labeling and grouping can have on children's self-image and attitudes toward school. Fortunately, most educators now recognize that more than a child's intelligence goes to school, and that tracking is flawed even in regard to intellectual achievement. The use of standardized test scores as a basis for tracking young students is now widely acknowledged to be unreliable, as well as harmful.

A particular danger is that the use of tracking has been found to be a "self-fulfilling prophecy," as most children know very well which group they have been placed in — no matter what it is called. Kids placed in the "dummy" class may simply assume that the adults' evaluation of them is correct, giving them little reason to try hard and a very good reason to hate school.

"As students pass the years organized in ways that separate them, they become polarized into pro- and anti-school camps that become increasingly estranged from one another (Gamoran and Berends 1987, p.426). One group achieves success in the classroom; the other finds success in the hallways and playgrounds."
- Paul George, *How to Untrack Your School*

Labels can last a lifetime

Even in schools where tracking is no longer used, the labeling of children continues in other ways, and the long-term effects of the labeling can be very destructive. Children who are labeled too early may internalize the labels and carry them around inside long after they have entered the adult world. Young children, in particular, are just beginning to develop a self-image through their interaction with peers and teachers, so they are particularly susceptible to others' evaluation of them.

Children, not unlike adults, do not easily forget humiliation and embarrassment. With their antennae attuned to the people they depend on, children are quick to perceive the disappointment felt by adults in their world. This is particularly true of children who are pushed into grades or programs before they are ready, and who are then labeled in ways which indicate they are not coping successfully. These children tend to accumulate feelings of inadequacy and self-doubt with surprising speed.

It is disturbing for a child to hear his or her name frequently mentioned by the teacher in a negative or nagging tone. Even worse, a child may hear a daily rendition of the same old theme: "You could do better if you would only try." Usually, the child is trying, if he or she hasn't yet given up, but effort alone is not enough to overcome the disadvantage of insufficient time to develop.

In another misguided attempt to spur a child on, a teacher may further damage a child's self-esteem by comparing the child with another student. And, a parent may do similar damage by comparing the child to a "successful" brother or sister. All too often, a child put in this situation sees the emphasis as being on the contrast between the two — the differences rather than the similarities — and assumes that he or she must be a "failure" if the other child is a "success."

A child can endure such a barrage of negative feedback for just so long before feeling totally defective as a person. The child is inclined to love and trust his parents and teachers. When he or she cannot please these significant adults, the response is likely to be, "There must be something wrong with me."

"In reality, a group of young children cannot all succeed when pressed to learn 'on schedule.' It is unrealistic and unfair to assume all the students in the same class will master the same concept or skill at the same time. They need to be allowed to acquire skills at their own individual pace."
- Anthony Coletta, Ph.D., *What's Best For Kids*

The child's feelings of inadequacy may be further reinforced when parents and teachers collaborate on ways to "correct" this "defective" student. Summer school, special programs, remedial reading, tutoring, language therapy, counseling — all these well-intentioned efforts to help the child may actually do further harm. These ancillary services usually result in some specific improvement in school performance, but they may also become a confirmation of the child's personal deficiency and unworthiness, especially if they end up being futile efforts which cannot provide what the child truly needs — extra time to grow and learn.

Similar negative feelings also tend to develop when a child is "socially promoted" year after year without having mastered the curriculum. Due to financial pressures and the ideological belief that any extra time is "retention" and therefore bad, some parents and educators claim that simply passing the child along from grade to grade will eventually solve whatever problems exist. However, the child, the other students, and the teacher all know that the child is in fact failing to learn what is needed and falling further behind. This knowledge — and the patterns it creates — eat away at the child's self-esteem, actual learning, and attitude towards school, while the endless wait continues year after year for the magic moment when the child will suddenly "catch up."

Failure on the installment plan

These sorts of negative experiences actually inhibit a child from trying and succeeding in school. One first grade teacher described the burden carried by a child in the wrong grade or program as an "emotional mortgage." Unfortunately, this sort of mortgage may never be paid off, because the initial experiences create expectations and patterns of behavior that repeat themselves over and over again in the years and decades that follow.

Some children, for example, exhibit what psychologists call "avoidance behavior," a fancy term for what most of us know as plain old procrastination. Children who choose procrastination as a survival technique — avoiding work, avoiding encounters, avoiding any kind of conflict or challenge — often continue this habit as adults, and thereby miss many opportunities for happiness.

Other survival methods that become ingrained in children through years of stress include fear of taking risks, nervousness, over-sensitivity, lack of confidence, lack of ease in social situations, aggressiveness, making excuses, and so on. Human nature being what it is, many people remain haunted by bad experiences they had in the early years — those ghosts from the past that taint our present and future. As a result of suffering exceptional stress during their primary education, some people never come close to realizing their potential as adults.

...many people remain haunted by bad experiences...

An adult who suffered and failed in school as a young child, and the parents of others like him, testify to the long-term negative effects of this experience:

"...how lonely I was. I was always too immature, both physically and emotionally, for the group I was with. Many of my social, personal, and even professional failures in adult life I lay to the fact that I went too fast, much too fast, all the way through school."

"My oldest son...started first grade when he was several months short of 6 years old...[The result was] years of constant struggle, inadequacy, frustration, and discouragement [which] finally caught up with Derrick in his junior and senior high school years...He is very self-deprecating and miserable...Here was a youngster of better-than-average intelligence...with a driving desire to measure up...crushed by twelve school years."

One of the saddest cases I have heard concerns a boy I shall call Timothy Brewster, who began having trouble in school while he was still in kindergarten. His mother was warned that Timmy would be kept back unless he could say the alphabet by April. Tim managed to pass because he learned the alphabet song, though he did not recognize the letters out of context. "If the teacher pointed to the letter E," his mother said, "he would hum the song until he got to E — only then could he identify the letter correctly."

"Timothy is being fired from first grade."

First grade was a disaster for Tim. He couldn't learn number concepts from ditto sheets — he needed hands-on materials — but his teacher didn't understand the underlying problem. She thought he was just being stubborn. By the end of the first term, Tim had collected 24 U's — for Unsatisfactory — on his report card. In addition to identifying Tim as an unsatisfactory 6-year-old, his report card also bore a note from the teacher that said, in effect, "Timothy is being fired from first grade."

Mrs. Brewster withdrew her son from first grade and placed him in a day-care center, because she had to work and the school did not have a kindergarten. "But, it took Tim years to recover from the pain he experienced in his first two years of school," his mother told me. "Ten years later, he still has trouble when he is presented with a new task or problem."

Childhood should be a journey, not a race

The public school system that is educating children today has probably changed greatly in many respects since you and I were in school, but it may not have changed at all in regard to its basic structure. Chances are you started kindergarten at age 5 and moved through the grades in lockstep with other children your age. A certain percentage of your classmates failed altogether, and others learned relatively little but were passed along from grade to grade, while most mastered the mandatory curriculum in the thirteen years until high school graduation.

Rather than forcing all students to master the same curriculum in the exact same amount of time — or become a "failure" — many schools now offer supportive extra-time options that allow children to learn well and experience success right from the start. These options may include a "readiness" year before kindergarten, a "transition" class after kindergarten, or a "multi-age" class lasting a few years. This last option enables children of different ages to learn and grow together over time — without being concerned about the artificial distinctions created by grade levels based on cut-off dates which may have nothing to do with a child's growth rate, or what the child is developmentally ready to learn.

By providing these sorts of options, schools can meet the needs of the full range of students entering each year. This approach recognizes that incoming children are ready to learn, want to learn, and can learn, as long as the material and teaching methods are appropriate for the children's developmental stage. And, it recognizes the importance of early intervention in helping children develop positive attitudes about learning and themselves, so they can achieve their full potential as students and as adults.

Does the concept of developmental readiness run counter to your personal history — to impressions you formed when you were very young about the way school is supposed to be? If so, this may make it difficult for you to accept the importance of readiness. And, with all the talk these days about the need for competitive advantages, you may feel you need to push children to proceed as quickly as possible with their education. In particular, many parents have been led to believe that the earlier children are introduced to academic subjects, the more successful they will be. However, the opposite is almost always the case.

The tortoise and the hare

Children learn and grow better when adults resist the current fashion to hurry children — to speed up their exposure to new concepts and experiences in an effort to help them get ahead of others, before they even know they're in a race. Extensive research and the experiences of many educators show that children need to progress through a particular stage of development at their own rate, in order to successfully complete the tasks of the next stage.

For example, kindergarten children who "play" with crayons, picture books, blocks, water, sand, and other hands-on objects are actually learning the rudiments of writing, reading, mathematics, physics, and other disciplines in an age-appropriate way. This prepares them to work with more abstract concepts like words and numbers when they are more mature. Children who are forced to memorize letters and numbers before they are developmentally ready lack the deeper understanding of the concepts behind these symbols, and so cannot work with them effectively.

Yet, today's parents are being told:

How To Teach Your Baby To Read,
How To Give Your Baby Encyclopedic
Knowledge,
How To Multiply Your Baby's Intelligence,
How To Raise A Brighter Child,
Kindergarten Is Too Late.

You might think I invented these phrases to ridicule what's happening today, but these are actual titles of books published for parents. These and other "quick fixes" are featured on television and radio and in the print media, where a weekly news magazine talks about "Bringing Up Super Baby," and a front-page newspaper photo shows 5-year-olds in caps and gowns on "Kindergarten Graduation Day."

Were any pseudo-experts able to make your baby girl walk before her muscles were ready to support her? Can they now accelerate the rate at which your son loses his baby teeth and replaces them with their successors. Not a chance. Yet, these rush-'em-into-reading experts claim they can turn your baby into a crawling encyclopedia, and that letting nature take its course is the road to disaster.

This sort of hurry-up hype is depriving children of their childhood. Not only is it detrimental to their mental and physical health, it may actually lead to long-term problems that prevent children from learning when and how they should.

"Throughout the 1980s and into the 1990s, many parents and even some teachers have unknowingly blocked progression through the stages of learning to read, by introducing phonics before children have demonstrated the ability to memorize and retell stories, as well as understand concepts about print."
- Anthony Coletta, Ph.D., *What's Best For Kids*

It is a terrible irony that some well-intentioned parents have actually set up their children to fail before the children even start kindergarten. And, other parents and educators make similar mistakes once children have entered school, by not allowing them to take the time they need to develop and succeed.

As children, many of us read the fable about the race between the tortoise and the hare. The hare sprinted far ahead early on, but it became so tired it eventually lost the race to the tortoise, which proceeded at the steady pace that matched its capabilities. Many of today's adults need to consider this fable and absorb its lessons, just as their children do. The following chapter provides a more detailed look at what happens to a child's education when these important lessons are ignored.

CHAPTER 3

Matt's Story: "He Still Needs To Learn Through Play"

"If at first you don't succeed, try, try again."
- an American proverb

o·ver·place (oh-ver-plays) *verb* 1. To assign a child to a grade, program, or curriculum which is inappropriate for the child's developmental level and/or academic level, resulting in harmful stress on the child that can eventually lead to school failure or marginal school performance.

Because his birthday is September 19th, Matthew Crane started school when he was 4-years-old. Where Matt lives, a child must be 5 by October 1st to enter kindergarten. Mr. and Mrs. Crane were pleased that their son was not excluded by the cut-off date, and that he had scored well on the cognitive examination administered to all incoming kindergarten students. They were proud of their boy, and he was excited about starting school.

On the first day of class, Matt clung to his mother when she started to leave. But, with a lot of coaxing, he was finally persuaded to stay. By the middle of the first week of kindergarten, he began to have stomach aches in the morning and to cry. Getting him off to school was a battle.

Matt's father and mother responded by pressuring him to go to school, believing they knew what was best for their son. They thought he would "grow out" of these problems. At the end of September, they were called to a conference with Matt's teacher.

"Matt is capable of doing the work," Ms. Watkins, the kindergarten teacher, said, "but he doesn't concentrate.

...he seems very young.

Instead, he wanders around the room bothering the other children. When I compare Matt to many of his classmates, he seems very young. He still needs to learn through play."

Mr. and Mrs. Crane were concerned, too. In the short time since Matt had started school, their enthusiastic and well-adjusted child had turned into a tense and tired complainer.

"Matt is exhausted when he gets home," his mother told Ms. Watkins. "He picks on his younger sister, because he's jealous that she can stay home. He complains all the time about school. And, he's having 'accidents' at night again — after staying dry for two years. Our pediatrician said the problem will go away once Matt gets used to school, but it hasn't. What can we do?"

Ms. Watkins recommended that Matt's parents move their child back to a pre-kindergarten program for young 5-year-olds, or keep him in the kindergarten class with the understanding that there would be an "adjustment" in the type of work Matt would be required to do. She added that the latter approach might lead to his spending two years in kindergarten.

Matt's parents opted for the second alternative, although they didn't want him to spend two years in kindergarten. And, at first their decision seemed to be the right one. At home, Matt stopped picking on his sister, stopped wetting his bed, and started sharing stories about school. At school, he completed some of his work and — more important to him — found a friend, someone he could swap food with at snack time and play with at recess. But, when it came time for "hard work," Matt always began to fidget, wanting to sharpen pencils or go to the bathroom or talk to his friend.

In the spring, Ms. Watkins told his parents that Matt should be "protected" from the requirements of first grade. She warned that if Matt were pushed ahead, he might have to repeat a grade at a later age, when it could be even more troubling for him. A "pre-first" program — which provided an extra year of continuous-progress, developmentally appropriate education between kindergarten and first grade — offered an alternative to moving directly to first grade, but the Cranes decided to risk it. They wanted to believe their son had made sufficient gains.

Matt's "graduation" from kindergarten was cause for rejoicing — he had made it! But, not for long.

Excerpts from Matthew Crane's School Record — Kindergarten

First term: Matt is one of the youngest children in the class. He accomplishes very little, though he's bright and very verbal. His immaturity is expressed in crying and an inability to stay on task.

Second term: Matt is very unhappy in a structured program. His parents feel school-related stress is at the root of some behavioral problems at home.

Third term: Adjusting the program has had a positive effect on Matt.

Fourth term: Matt continues to improve, but because we adjusted the program, he has not mastered the necessary concepts and skills required for a successful first grade placement. I strongly recommend that Matt be placed in a pre-first grade transition class.

Grade assignment: At his parents' request, Matt is promoted to first grade.

In September, Matt was assigned to an experienced teacher, Mrs. Flagg, a veteran of 22 years. Matt's dad told the principal, "We want him with Mrs. Flagg. If anyone can make him do the work, she can." Matt's anxiety level was high as he remembered what had happened at this time last year, but he went willingly off to school on the first day.

Mrs. Flagg knew that Matt needed monitoring, so she seated him near the front of the class. He liked sitting close to her desk, where he could see the pictures in the books she read to the class every day. What he disliked was sitting near two girls who were nearly a year older than he was, and who seemed a whole lot smarter. They actually loved school!

First grade became harder and harder...

First grade became harder and harder for Matt. At home, he burst into tears over the least little thing. One evening, he confided to his mother that he wasn't as smart as the other children. His mother tenderly assured him that he was very smart — he just needed "to try a little harder," and soon he would catch up with the rest. Inwardly, Matt's mother sighed. What had happened to this child, who had been so quick to learn and so filled with energy and confidence before he entered school?

Mrs. Flagg initiated a conference. "Matthew is certainly intelligent," she said, "but at this stage of his development he is not ready for the type of work required in first grade."

Matt's parents were not ready to accept what Mrs. Flagg told them. Surely, they pleaded, if they cooperated with the school, if they worked with Matt at home, if they put him to bed earlier, if they took away his TV privileges, if they were all tougher on him — surely then Matt would succeed. Mrs. Flagg disagreed, but when his parents resisted her recommendation that Matt's grade placement be changed, she agreed to "sit on Matt."

Once again, things were on the upswing — temporarily. Closely monitored and kept under constant pressure, Matt could accomplish average work. He liked receiving extra help, but he knew he wasn't doing as well as expected. Sometimes, the harder he tried, the more mistakes he made. That made him feel helpless and stupid. Sometimes, he just didn't want to try at all.

In March, Mr. and Mrs. Crane heard exactly what they did not want to hear. Mrs. Flagg wanted to retain Matt. She thought his self-concept — already low — might suffer even more if he were promoted and had to spend another year trying to catch up.

Matt's parents were concerned about his self-concept, too. "If he's left back, he'll really feel like a failure," his mother said. "And, he'll miss his friends terribly."

"Why not try him in second grade?" his father asked. "Then, if he doesn't knuckle down, we might make him repeat a grade."

Against Mrs. Flagg's recommendation, Matt was promoted "on trial." His parents agreed that he would finish first grade over the summer, which made Matt feel cheated. Now, he had to spend his vacation on all that stuff he hated most — math, phonics, and reading. At 6-years-old, life wasn't fair.

Excerpts From Matthew Crane's School Record — Grade One

First term: Matthew has a good grasp of number and letter concepts but is unable to concentrate. He seems exceptionally young for first grade, showing little interest in pencil/paper tasks.

Second term: Matthew's work habits are inconsistent; he does well one day, poorly the next two. I'm referring him for special help in reading three days a week and tutoring twice a week.

Third term: Still very young and sometimes very unhappy, Matthew has a poor self-concept. A good candidate for two years in first grade.

Fourth term: Matthew is not doing the sort of work that will allow him to succeed in second grade. I recommend that he spend another year in first grade.

Grade assignment: Promoted to grade two on trial. Parents are obliged to see that he completes grade one work before September.

Within two weeks after school opened, Mr. and Mrs. Crane sensed that a storm was brewing. Their son complained, "Ms. Carmen teaches too fast; she never explains things; she doesn't give me enough time."

Early in October, they met with the teacher, whose concerns sounded like accusations:

"Matt rarely completes his work...He doesn't follow instructions well...His verbal self-defense borders on backtalk...His attention span is very short...He once tore up a paper in frustration...He has behaved aggressively toward other children..."

Mr. and Mrs. Crane were devastated. Maybe there was something wrong with the school, they thought, or with the teacher — maybe the teacher didn't like Matt. They requested a meeting with the principal, guidance counselor, and teacher, during which all agreed to have Matt evaluated.

To no one's surprise, an intelligence test showed that Matt's I.Q. was well above average, even though he was about six months behind academically. The assessment of his developmental level indicated that he was not yet ready for his current grade placement. The principal recommended that Matt take two years to complete second grade.

Matt's dad replied firmly, "We've made a tremendous investment of time and energy in Matt's education. I can't see letting him flunk now. The tests show how intelligent he is. My son is not going to be held back — except as a very last resort. Can't you people come up with an acceptable alternative?"

Ms. Carmen then devised an individual plan for Matt. Each week, the boy signed a "contract" outlining tasks to be done, with rewards and consequences built in. The guidance counselor, Mr. Hall, met with the boy once a week.

To everyone's relief, this rigid structure seemed to help Matt succeed. At great personal expense, he finished enough of the second grade curriculum to be promoted. Sadly, he brought home math, phonics, and reading material when school closed for the summer. His schedule allowed little time for play.

His schedule allowed little time for play.

Excerpts from Matthew Crane's School Record —
Grade Two

First term: Matthew is over his head, unable to follow directions or finish work. His behavior reveals significant frustration.

Second term: Matthew was referred for further testing. Results indicate that he's developmentally young, despite superior intelligence. He'll receive tutoring and special reading help. Mr. Hall will shore up his confidence.

Third term: Matt is under contract to carry out an individualized instructional plan in math and language arts.

Fourth term: Matt is able to function only when under pressure. He has completed the minimal requirements of second grade.

Grade assignment: Promoted to third grade. Summer study "a must."

On the opening day of classes, it was Matt's mother's turn to cry, as she watched him go off to school. He had just promised her, "I'm really going to try hard this year. I won't be bad any more." Forcing Matt to go to school like this just isn't right, Mrs. Crane thought. My boy is really hurting.

Minutes after Matt reached school that morning, he listened to Mrs. Brennan outline her plans for the year, and he knew he was in deep trouble.

"As third graders, you will learn to tell time to the minute (no digital watches allowed)! You will use cursive lettering without mixing in manuscript letters... you will make a monthly book report...you will have homework...you will work independently...you must copy accurately from the board...and you will learn your multiplication tables for 0–12 by June!"

When Matt came home that day, his mother took one look at him and knew the whole story. He ran to her in tears. "I'll never be able to do all the stupid third grade work! Third grade is dumb." Mrs. Crane held Matt close. I'm always pushing him and pushing him, she thought, and it's just too hard for him. Maybe we are making a serious mistake in sending Matt to third grade.

That evening, Matt's mother shared her concerns with her husband, but he saw moving his son back a grade as a personal defeat for himself. "Look," he said, "set up an appointment with Mrs. Brennan, and we'll see what she has to say about Matt."

When they met with Mrs. Brennan, she was thoroughly familiar with Matt's school history — his situation was well-documented. Even so, she believed she could help him "get through" third grade. Reluctantly, Matt's mother agreed with the decision to keep Matt where he was.

Despite everyone's best efforts, Matt fell further and further behind. For his parents, life seemed to drag along from one school conference to the next. They wondered if they had failed their son. They wondered how long they could endure the nightly tussles with homework.

Matt fell further and further behind.

In December, Matt's parents were invited to an evening meeting, sponsored by the PTA, on the subject of school success and school failure. There, they heard a speaker outline the concepts of developmental readiness and proper grade placement, and they listened as parents whose children had taken extra time endorsed this approach enthusiastically.

After the meeting, Mrs. Crane said firmly, "I know that Matt belongs in second grade."

"Those other kids probably aren't as smart as Matt," Mr. Crane said. "Matt's working really hard right now. I think I can keep after him enough so that he will make it through third, and I want to try a little longer." Deep down, however, Mr. Crane suspected that his wife was right, and that he was wrong in stubbornly forcing Matt to work way over his head.

For Matt, recess was the only thing that made school endurable. There, he played with second graders and felt they were his real friends. One January morning, he asked if he could spend the day with his "old" second grade teacher, Mrs. Carmen. After first checking with her, Mrs. Brennan granted his request.

After school that day, Matt talked non-stop about the great time he'd had in school and how easy it was. For

For once, he could finish his assignments.

once, he felt like one of the smartest kids in the class. For once, he could finish his assignments.

At the supper table, his father was stunned as he listened to son's enthusiasm for school bubbling over. "Can I go back to Mrs. Carmen's class again next week?" Matt asked.

There was silence at the table as Mr. Crane considered his son's request. Matt's happiness was so evident that Mr. Crane's resistance finally crumbled. "Matt, let me ask you something," Mr. Crane said very seriously. "Would you like to finish this school year back in second grade, in Mrs. Carmen's class?"

Would he! Four years of accumulated failure seemed to lift off Matt's shoulders as his father spoke, but then the boy hesitated and said softly, "The other kids are going make fun of me if I go back to second grade. They think I'm stupid, any way."

Mr. Crane promised that he and Matt's mother would help Matt learn how to talk about the change, and that they would have the school principal, teachers, and guidance counselor speak to the other children.

With the same determination that he had insisted on Matt's staying in third grade, Mr. Crane supported the decision to move back a grade, now certain it was really a step forward. And, Matt knew — from his father's tone and his mother's smile — that he had the support of the people who were most important in his world.

The next day, it was surprisingly easy to have Matt move back to second grade. Mrs. Brennan hoped his parents wouldn't blame her for putting too much pressure on Matt. Mrs. Carmen was delighted to have him in her class again, and she wished she had pushed harder to keep him. Mr. Hall spoke to the second and third graders, saying it was perfectly all right for a boy or girl to take extra time in school. Because Betty,

Mike, and Jamie were also taking an extra year in second grade, the situation was somewhat easier for Matt.

Matt did have to take some teasing from the other children, but because his parents had prepared him and because he was so relieved to be out of the hopeless situation in third grade, it didn't bother him as much as he expected. When Lance, a third grader, purposely bumped into him on the playground and said, "Get out of my way, dummy," Matt just said to himself, "I'm not going to let this bother me too much. I know it wasn't my fault that I couldn't do the work in third grade, and I like being in second grade. My mother and my teacher both told me that I'm not stupid. My report card from now on will show everybody that I'm smart."

Matt's mother had explained to him that his trouble in school was not his fault — and never had been his fault. She blamed herself and his father for making him try to do work he wasn't ready for. Their intention was good — after all, don't most parents start their children in school when the school officials tell them to, even if the children are only 4-years-old? But, they made a mistake by insisting that he keep moving up a grade each year, even though he hadn't really completed the one he was in. Now, they were asking him to help correct the mistake. And, they wanted to make sure he knew that they loved him very much.

Excerpts from Matthew Crane's School Record — Grades 3 & 2

First term: Matt has a defeatist attitude and seems totally overwhelmed. He lacks the academic skills and level of maturity to handle third grade.

Second term: Matt's parents are supportive and work with him every night, but Matt is still far behind.

Third term: Matt has been re-entered in grade two and is much happier. His parents report he's like "a new child" at home. He now ranks in the top third of his class and shows few signs of the problems he had exhibited in the past.

Fourth term: Matt's best term ever. He has completed all of his assignments. His work shows care. He has emerged as a class leader, showing initiative.

Grade assignment: Matt is promoted to grade three unconditionally.

Living "happily ever after..." (with a few exceptions)

Matt no longer dreaded bringing home his report cards, and his parents no longer had to "chain him down" to do his homework. He had time to play after school, and the Cranes' refrigerator became so plastered with Matt's school work that it looked like the supermarket bulletin board.

Some things take more time to work out, however. Children who are over their heads in school develop poor work habits that are reinforced as they move up through the grades. Matt, for example, had developed the habit of frequently asking for directions to be repeated. This habit originated from his restlessness, which made it hard for him to listen, and from the fact that asking a question often worked as a stalling tactic, keeping him from having to deal immediately with his work. Habits are hard to break, and it took a couple of years before Matt was able — nearly always — to listen well the first time around.

In addition, during his first attempt at third grade, he had developed a need to disappear into the bathroom whenever the teacher announced math work. Little by little, over time, Matt was able to overcome this habit, too. His self-confidence was on the upswing.

By the time he reached the upper elementary school grades, Matt's poor work habits and signs of stress had all but vanished. A trace of his early experience lingered on in his answer when someone innocently asked him which grade he was in. Like many other children who have taken more than one year to complete a grade, Matt invariably replied, "I'm in the sixth grade, but I'm supposed to be in seventh." This is the apology of a child who has felt like a failure — a child who needs to hear, "You are right where you are supposed to be."

Mr. and Mrs. Crane have not yet fully recovered from the trauma of their boy's start in school, and they probably never will. His mother occasionally looks at Matt and wonders to herself, "Why didn't I listen to him and my own concerns when Matt so clearly communicated how he felt that first year in school? How could I have failed to understand that Matt wasn't physically ready to do some activities for long periods of time...or socially ready to share his teacher with all the other children...or emotionally ready to handle this sort of pressure? Now, I can easily understand the concept of developmental readiness, but when we were all swept up in the situation, I thought, 'he's the right age to be in school, he's intelligent, and he'll soon outgrow these problems.' It took so long to see that he was truly too young, and we jeopardized his entire future by pressuring him."

he was truly too young

Matt's father sometimes thinks, "Was it my stiff-necked pride that made me insist for so long on Matt's not taking extra time? Was it my fear of what my father would think of his grandson? Or, was it my real concern for the boy? I remember when I was in school — how fearful I was of being left back, and how relieved I was to be promoted when those report cards were issued at the end of the year. And, how mean we were to the kids who didn't make it. Now, I understand

"From now on, my boy's true needs come first."

how unimportant all of that is. Who cares what some people think about Matt's grade placement, as long as he's happy and successful? From now on, my boy's true needs come first."

Rewriting the past — and the future

By the time Matt's younger brother — who was born in July — was old enough to enter kindergarten, the school had several extra-time options available that offered supportive, continuous-progress alternatives. And, having learned from their first son's experiences, the Cranes responded positively and without hesitation to the recommendation that their younger son take the extra time needed to experience school success right from the start.

Had Matt been placed properly in school right at the beginning — based on his developmental stage, rather than just his chronological age — his introduction to school would have been a much more positive experience, and each succeeding year another building block for future success. Children's initial placement in school is far too important to be determined just by the number of candles on their birthday cakes.

CHAPTER 4
What "School Stress" Looks Like: Signs And Signals That Children Need Help

"Neglected developmental needs fester, creating problems in learning."
- Priscilla Vail, *Emotion: The On/Off Switch for Learning*

With their bodies, their gestures, and their facial expressions — not just their words — children communicate their needs. For example, any parent knows what it means when a child's bottom lip begins to quiver. And, most teachers and parents recognize a variety of ways children indicate they are feeling happy or sad, energetic or exhausted, full of mischief or miserable. Children constantly make statements about themselves through their behavior.

Even when children try to conceal their feelings, they usually are not very good at it. Without meaning to, they "give away" their intentions through their body language, letting parents and teachers pick up the cues. These silent signals are often calls for help, but occasionally society's expectations may blind us to the messages a child is transmitting.

This chapter can help you train yourself to recognize the signals of children placed in the wrong grade or program at school. Remember that recognizing the distress of such children is the first step toward extricating them from a bad situation, and placing them where they belong.

A "One-Size-Fits-All" Approach

Children in kindergarten or first grade come in a great variety of shapes and sizes — tall, short, plump, lean, large, medium, small. Can you imagine the principal of a school ignoring all of these physical differences and insisting that all children in first grade wear the same size shoes?

The way you fit into your shoes and the way you fit into a school both affect your growth and comfort when you are young. Shoes that don't fit can cause considerable damage — they hurt children physically, contribute to emotional and social discomfort, distract children intellectually, and might just affect the way a child walks through the rest of his or her life. Proper-fitting shoes give their wearer a firm and secure basis for proceeding, just as the proper fit in a grade or program gives a student a solid educational foundation.

Of course, no school principal would consider forcing 6-year-olds to all wear the same size shoe. But, when it comes to primary education, some administrators adopt just such a "one-size-fits-all" approach, leaving some mismatched children with permanent scars.

...class sizes have increased in many schools...

The rationale for taking this approach is that a kindergarten or primary grade teacher can simply "individualize the instruction." Unfortunately, however, class sizes have increased in many schools, at the same that children's natural diversity — their differing interests, talents, academic achievements, developmental stages and cultural backgrounds — is being further complicated by the "full inclusion" of severely handicapped children who previously would have been in small special education classes taught by teachers prepared specifically to work with such children. In addition, the "standards" and "mandates" being legislated in many states require the teachers to cram even more curriculum and instruction into the same school year.

Under these circumstances, a teacher would have to be a wiz of a wizard to provide individualized instruction to such a wide range of children, and have them all attain the same educational goals in the exact same amount of time. While most teachers actually accomplish an amazing amount during the school year, there are some things even they cannot do. No matter how much a teacher pushes or individualizes, no matter how much pressure the parents exert, no matter how malleable the children, they simply cannot all be forced to develop and learn at the same rate. And, the reality is that kids "get all bent out of shape" when their developmental and educational needs are not met.

Train yourself to be
a "stress detector"

Children who wear the wrong size shoes compensate by walking in distorted ways. Similarly, children who are in the wrong grade or program respond in ways that will help them survive the experience, but that interfere with their capacity to lead happy, productive lives. While their lives are being distorted in this way, their bodies and/or emotions often exhibit signs that indicate the children are experiencing too much stress and need adult help.

While you can train yourself to detect signs of stress in children, it is not always easy to interpret their meaning. But, if you suspect that a child is in the wrong grade or program, and you then notice that the child frequently exhibits signs of stress, that observation reinforces what you have suspected in your heart all along: the child is in deep water and may be sinking fast.

Think of stress signs as clues — possible indicators that a child is developmentally too young for the demands of a particular grade or program. Remember, however, that all children display some signs of stress from time to time. The real clues to serious trouble are consistency and multiplicity. If a child *continually* exhibits *several* stress signs over an *extended* period, then it is time to take action.

Remember, too, that children who are Learning Disabled and children who are in the wrong grade or program may exhibit identical signs of stress. In fact, some children who have been identified as "educationally handicapped" turned out to be "educationally superior" when provided with an appropriate placement and an opportunity to develop at their own rate. And, some students who seem to have an Attention Deficit Disorder may really be having trouble concentrating because they are developmentally too young for the curriculum and/or method of instruction.

The signs of stress found in the next few pages are organized into three different groups:

developmental stress signs — physical, emotional, social, intellectual

"covert" stress signs

stress signs by age level

These different perspectives are not meant to be mutually exclusive; they should be used together to obtain an understanding of the "whole child." Start by reading through the next several pages, keeping in mind that a child need only show a few of these signs to indicate the possibility of trouble, and that children who consistently exhibit these signs are likely to be in trouble at home as well as in school, which compounds the amount of stress they experience.

Listen carefully to such a child and watch for behavior patterns. As you do, trust your own innate common sense and good judgement. Let your understanding of the child guide you in making the tough decisions likely to shape the child's life.

Developmental stress signs

Children's physical, emotional, social, and intellectual growth are four key aspects of their overall development. And, children who are developmentally too young for a particular grade or program may exhibit their unhappiness through any or all four of these aspects. The signs and signals in this section have been compiled into "portraits" which may help you identify particular students in need of help. The portraits will also help you understand how children in the wrong grade or program latch on to certain stratagems in order to survive the misery of being mismatched in school.

Children showing signs of physical stress

Frowning, squinting, a clenched jaw...this sort of facial expression reflects a child's misery in school. He or she may also appear to be burdened by "the weight of the world" on hunched shoulders.

A child of this sort often hears everything going on inside (and outside) the classroom — except the teacher's instructions. The child may hear only the last half of the instructions, or may insist, "The teacher never told us to do that." He or she frequently needs to have directions repeated again and again — and again.

Daily demands which cannot be met take their toll on children. Some may miss school frequently because of exhaustion. Others fall asleep during afternoon story time or need after-school naps.

Daily demands which cannot be met take their toll...

Too much stress may also result in low resistance to illness. First graders in particular seem pre-disposed to morning stomach aches and colds.

For overplaced children, school is frequently a physical struggle. Their writing is laborious; they quickly grow tired; they cannot sit through a twenty-minute reading lesson, much less a five-hour day. Often, they will try to negotiate: "Hey, teacher, can I write just a little bit and not the whole sentence?"

Some of these children learn to hate writing — with good reason. Their fine-motor control skills are not yet fully developed, so they take too long to complete written assignments, they make holes in the paper from constant erasing, and they mix cursive and manuscript writing, as well as capital and lower case letters.

...writing is so difficult it literally hurts.

For these children, writing is so difficult it literally hurts.

Reading tends to be difficult for developmentally young children as well, so they try to avoid both reading and writing whenever they can. When they must read and/or write, they may invert, reverse, omit, and substitute letters and words.

Children showing signs of emotional stress

These children constantly seek adult approval and reassurance. Too filled with self-doubt to work independently, they want and need a lot of praise for each little effort they make.

The child who always has to know "right now" if he's "right," even when it means interrupting the teacher, has a tremendous fear of making a mistake. This extreme concern about being right prevents the child from taking risks — even from volunteering answers. Living like a second-class citizen, he or she often does not have the confidence to try new endeavors.

Children who are overplaced in a grade or program often lose their place in a lesson and give the right answer to the wrong question — their bodies are there, but their minds have "gone fishing." Put another way, recurrent daydreaming becomes an escape mechanism that helps emotionally stressed children get through the day.

Always on the go, this sort of child needs constant physical movement to release tension. He or she is easily distracted and loves "in-house field trips" to the pencil sharpener. If allowed, the child would make ten trips a day to visit/help the school custodian. (Adults may suspect the child of having an Attention Deficit Disorder, when in fact the problem is incorrect placement in a grade or program.)

At the same time, this child often lacks confidence in his or her physical ability to measure up to other children. Fearful of getting hurt, he or she may avoid contact sports. If the fear is strong enough, the child may complain when accidently touched by another student. Sometimes picked on by classmates, this child feels inferior and suffers from low self-esteem.

A child experiencing emotional stress also cries easily, because crying helps to release tension. When school work seems too hard, or when the child is scolded or otherwise feels threatened, tears may quickly appear, revealing how young the child truly is. Transitions and social situations are especially difficult for this child to handle.

Nailbiting may also occur, as having a hand in the mouth aids a nervous child in "handling" anxiety. Other signs of nervousness include frequent throat clearing, coughing, eye blinking, and bed wetting.

Children in the wrong grade or program may behave very well at school but very badly at home, though their home behavior improves during school holidays and vacations. The difference in home and school behavior is so marked, parents may think they are hearing a case of mistaken identity when the teacher describes their own child. In reality, the child's emotional repression at school is resulting in extensive emotional release at home.

Children showing signs of social stress
These children stay on the sidelines, avoiding other children. They do not seem to fit in with their peer group, and often feel unaccepted and rejected.

A child who feels pushed aside in school may push back at others in retaliation, or "act up" in ways that are annoying. Hurt and left out, the child sometimes lashes out in anger and jealousy at successful classmates. He or she may become a bully, obtaining attention — even though it's negative — and demonstrating a superiority over the other kids in at least one respect.

This child actually feels smaller and weaker than others his age. Having few friends and not knowing what others expect, he or she feels uncomfortable in social situations. He may seek out younger children because his interests are like theirs, and he is likely to enjoy visiting a grade lower than his own. She would rather play alone than take chances competing.

In order to survive in school, these children invent reasons for their not meeting expectations: "The teacher said it wasn't due today," "I did the work last night but forgot to bring it to school," "Someone must have taken my homework."

Passive and apathetic, this sort of child takes no initiative in class, drifting along with what others do. At home, the child's favorite activity is watching television.

Children showing signs of intellectual stress

These children do very well one day, but poorly the next. Brains are not their problem — they tend to be bright but too young developmentally to keep up the pace. They therefore use their intellectual powers to create endless excuses for missing or incomplete work.

Constantly playing "catch up," these children cannot complete their work in a reasonable amount of time, because they are unable to stay on task. Instead, they are the first to let the rest of the class know when it's time for recess or lunch.

Parents may blame the teacher for "not challenging" the child, who claims that school is "too easy" or "boring." The truth, however, is that the pressure is too much for the child. It might even lead to a "lost" or altered report card.

"She has the potential but won't apply herself." "He could do the work, but he's just plain lazy." When parents or teachers find themselves saying things like this at a school conference, it's an indication that the real problem may be a lack of readiness.

...the real problem may be a lack of readiness.

Children who don't make waves may still need rescuing

Every child who is experiencing school stress does not behave exactly like every other child in a similar situation, but all such children do exhibit signs that something is wrong. The way a particular child reveals feelings of stress depends upon his or her individual personality, as well as upon family upbringing and the classroom environment. Some children who feel oppressed by school react *overtly*, clearly showing the stress they feel. Other children become withdrawn and express their distress in a *covert* manner. In either case, what the child is experiencing is very painful and very real.

Some children who appear to be passive or "too good to be true" may really feel too frightened and vulnerable to reveal themselves. The resulting covert stress signs present a particular challenge to adults, because these signs are difficult to detect, let alone interpret.

Certain types of children under stress are more likely to show their unhappiness in covert ways. These include:

children who are intellectually very bright but immature in their social, emotional, or physical development;

girls who have been raised in the "good little girl" tradition;

children who have been under undue pressure to perform and succeed;

"hurried" children who take on adult roles.

Here are some examples of covert behavior, which can help you recognize when such a child is under stress:

a child who is apathetic, passive, unresponsive, or ultra-obedient;

a child who seems bored, unmotivated, or just "goes through the motions;"

a child who does little but read or who focuses exclusively on academic study;

a child who seldom participates in class or other activities, striving to go unnoticed;

a child who talks "a blue streak" but avoids writing;

a child who avoids challenge and competition;

a child who often postpones work.

Age-level checklists of school stress signs and signals

Children who are in the wrong grade or program typically display certain signs and signals of stress at each age level. Some of the signs are unique to particular ages; other signs — such as "develops a nervous tic" — span several ages.

As you review the checklists, you may "recognize" one or more children who have reached the age indicated and display signs or signals for that age. A child who displays only a few of these behavior patterns may be under considerable stress. Do remember, though, that all children occasionally fit some of the descriptions. It is only when a child consistently displays several signs of stress for an extended period of time that adults need to be concerned.

Many educators have found these checklists to be a helpful framework for observing children and discussing individual children with their parents. For these purposes, the checklists for 4, 5 and 6-year-olds can be obtained separately in a format suitable for individual use. In particular, space is provided to note whether the specific behaviors *never* occur, *rarely* occur, or *often* occur. Analyzing the frequency of behaviors in this way can help to determine the overall severity of a child's school stress.

4-Year-Olds: Signs and signals of preschool stress

At Home

A 4-year-old suffering from preschool-related stress may:

1. not want to leave Mom/Dad;
2. hide shoes so as not to have to go to preschool;
3. complain about stomach aches or headaches;
4. have bathroom "accidents;"
5. come home exhausted;
6. have nightmares.

At Preschool

A 4-year-old experiencing the stress of being in the wrong group or program may:

1. have difficulty separating from Mom/Dad;
2. cling to the teacher, showing a high degree of dependency;
3. not participate in "cooperative" play — instead, his or her play is "isolated" (child plays alone) or "parallel" (playing next to other children but not with them);
4. not like the other children;
5. show "young" fine-motor coordination while cutting, gluing, drawing, etc.;
6. demonstrate a lack of awareness of appropriate behavior in the "classroom;"
7. not catch on to "classroom" routines, which more mature classmates adapt to easily;
8. find it difficult to select activities and stick with them;
9. become "outspoken" and/or want to leave when asked to perform a task that is too difficult.

In General

A 4-year-old who is under an excessive amount of stress at preschool may:

1. cry easily;
2. lack self-control or self-discipline (biting, hitting and kicking);
3. appear to be "shy;"
4. revert to thumbsucking, nailbiting, or "baby talk;"
5. become aggressive during games and other activities involving the taking of turns or sharing.

Note: All children display some stress signs at times. Severe stress is indicated when a child consistently displays several stress signs over an extended period of time.

5-Year-Olds: Signs and signals of school stress

At Home
A 5-year-old suffering from school-related stress may:

1. not want to leave Mom/Dad;
2. not want to go to school;
3. suffer from stomach aches or headaches, particularly in the morning before school;
4. dislike school or complain that school is "dumb;"
5. complain that the teacher does not allow enough time to finish his or her school work;
6. need to rest, but resist taking a nap;
7. revert to bedwetting.

At School
A 5-year-old experiencing the stress of being in the wrong grade or program may:

1. show little interest in kindergarten "academics;"
2. frequently ask if it's time to go home;
3. be unable to hold scissors as directed by the teacher;
4. worry that Mom will forget to pick him or her up after school;
5. have a difficult time following the daily routine;
6. talk incessantly;
7. complain that school work is "too hard" ("I can't do it,") or "too easy" ("It's so easy, I'm not going to do it,") or "too boring;"
8. interrupt the teacher constantly;
9. be unable to shift easily from one task to the next;
10. be overly restless during class, and frequently in motion when supposed to be working at a task.

In General
A 5-year-old who is under an excessive amount of
stress at school may:

1. become withdrawn;
2. revert to thumbsucking or infantile speech;
3. compare herself negatively to other children
   ("They can do it, but I can't.");
4. complain that he has no friends;
5. cry easily and frequently;
6. make up stories;
7. bite his or her nails;
8. seem depressed.

Note: All children display some stress signs at times.
Severe stress is indicated when a child consistently
displays several stress signs over an extended period of
time.

6-Year-Olds: Signs and signals of school stress

At Home

A 6–year-old suffering from school-related stress may:

1. frequently complain of before-school stomach aches;
2. revert to bed-wetting;
3. behave in a manner that seems out of character to the parent or teacher;
4. frequently ask to stay at home.

At School

A 6–year-old experiencing the stress of being in the wrong grade or program may:

1. prefer to play with younger children;
2. want to play with toys during class time;
3. choose recess, gym, and music as favorite subjects;
4. feel overwhelmed by the size and activity level of the lunchroom;
5. have a high rate of absenteeism;
6. try to take frequent "in-house field trips" to the pencil sharpener, bathroom, school nurse, custodian, etc.;
7. mark papers randomly;
8. "act out" on the playground;
9. reverse, invert, substitute, or omit letters and numbers when reading and/or writing (this is also not unusual for properly placed students, either);
10. complain about being bored with school work, when in reality he or she cannot do the work;
11. have a short attention span — be unable to stay focused on a twenty-minute reading lesson;
12. have difficulty understanding the teacher's instructions.

In General

A 6-year-old who is under an excessive amount of stress at school may:

1. cry easily and frequently;
2. tire quickly;
3. need constant reassurance and praise;
4. become withdrawn and shy;
5. develop a nervous tic — a twitching eye, a nervous cough, frequent clearing of the throat or twirling of hair;
6. revert to thumbsucking;
7. lie or "adjust the truth" about school;
8. revert to soiling his or her pants;
9. make restless body movements, such as rocking in a chair, jiggling legs, etc.;
10. dawdle;
11. seem depressed;
12. feel harried/hurried.

Note: All children display some stress signs at times. Severe stress is indicated when a child consistently displays several stress signs over an extended period of time.

7-Year-Olds: Signs and signals of school stress

At Home

A 7-year-old suffering from school-related stress may:

1. develop a psychosomatic illness, such as a stomach ache, a headache, a sore leg, a limp, a "temp," etc.;
2. wet the bed or soil his/her pants;
3. develop a well-founded fear of going on to third grade;
4. frequently ask to stay at home.

At School

A 7-year-old experiencing the stress of being in the wrong grade or program may:

1. prefer playing with younger children;
2. constantly erase his or her work (many 7-year-olds do a great deal of erasing);
3. try to create diversions from the work at hand;
4. frequently be absent;
5. act aggressively on the playground;
6. develop poor work habits, such as ripping up papers, losing papers, keeping a messy desk;
7. have difficulty staying with a task or lesson;
8. revert, invert, substitute, or omit letters and numbers when reading and/or writing;
9. feel badgered about reading;
10. be "consistently inconsistent" about work;
11. focus exclusively on one subject, such as math, and have no interest in other subjects.

In General
A 7-year-old who is under an excessive amount of
stress at school may:

1. cry easily;
2. "stretch" the truth;
3. withdraw;
4. develop a nervous tic — a twitching eye, a nervous
   cough, frequent clearing of the throat or twirling
   of hair, etc.;
5. pull out his or her hair;
6. seem depressed;
7. complain about "everything."

Note: All children display some stress signs at times.
Severe stress is indicated when a child consistently
displays several stress signs over an extended period of
time.

8-Year-Olds: Signs and signals of school stress

At Home
An 8-year-old suffering from school-related stress may:

1. complain about "too much" school work;
2. pick on siblings;
3. develop a psychosomatic illness, such as a stomach ache, a headache, a sore leg, a limp, a "temp," etc.;
4. be difficult to direct.

At School
An 8-year-old experiencing the stress of being in the wrong grade or program may:

1. prefer to play with younger children;
2. dislike certain subjects (which means she may know she's behind and doesn't know how to do the work);
3. write laboriously and find cursive writing extremely difficult;
4. feel overwhelmed by the volume of work;
5. seem incapable of working independently;
6. ask for permission to visit previous grade;
7. frequently say, "My old teacher did it this way;"
8. find that even a reasonable amount of copying from the chalkboard is extremely difficult;
9. be unable to memorize the multiplication tables;
10. habitually lose or destroy papers;
11. find shifting to hardcover textbooks extremely difficult.

In General

An 8-year-old who is under an excessive amount of stress at school may:

1. cherish toys and make them more important during class time than is appropriate for his or her age;
2. develop a nervous tic — a twitching eye, a nervous cough, frequent clearing of the throat or twirling of hair;
3. not seem to fit into his or her peer group;
4. take out frustrations on other children during play;
5. be picked on or rejected by peers, and called names such as "dumb," "stupid," "airhead," etc.;
6. have difficulty learning to tell time and prefer to wear a digital watch;
7. chew on pencils, buttons, collars, or whatever is handy;
8. find change threatening and have difficulty handling new situations.

Note: All children display some stress signs at times. Severe stress is indicated when a child consistently displays several stress signs over an extended period of time.

9-Year-Olds: Signs and signals of school stress

At Home
A 9-year-old suffering from school-related stress may:

1. demand excessive assistance with homework, thus causing family tension;
2. express fear about going on to the next grade.

At School
A 9-year-old experiencing the stress of being in the wrong grade or program may:

1. prefer playing with younger children;
2. often mix manuscript and cursive writing (some mixing is normal);
3. observe what is happening elsewhere in the classroom, rather than focusing on the work at hand;
4. complete only parts of assignments;
5. look for excuses to leave the classroom ("May I go to the lunch room and find out what's on the menu?");
6. be the last one chosen for team games and sports;
7. need to be taught the same concepts again and again — for example, he or she may need the rules of division, capitalization, and punctuation repeated frequently, and then will forget them again over the weekend or during a vacation period.
8. be unable to memorize the multiplication and/or division tables, and so need to keep sneaking peeks at the charts;
9. constantly break pencils, necessitating extra trips to the pencil sharpener;
10. be unable to locate pencils, pens, papers, and books in his or her own desk;
11. forget how to "set up" a paper with name, date, subject, and margins;
12. copy another child's work when under extreme pressure;
13. "trail" the teacher around the classroom.

In General
A 9-year-old who is under excessive stress at school
may:

1. need an abundance of supervision and reassurance;
2. not work well independently;
3. develop a preoccupation with "being right;"
4. procrastinate and avoid work;
5. daydream frequently;
6. develop a nervous tic — a twitching eye, a nervous
   cough, frequent clearing of the throat or twirling
   of hair;
7. seem depressed.

Note: All children display some stress signs at times.
Severe stress is indicated when a child consistently
displays several stress signs over an extended period of
time.

10-Year-Olds: Signs and signals of school stress

At School

A 10-year-old experiencing the stress of being in the wrong grade or program may:

1. prefer to play with younger children;
2. have great difficulty with abstractions in math, such as division, fractions, and geometry;
3. enjoying playing with clay, erasers, rubber bands, and tape, and keep on the desk such "toys" as fancy erasers, homemade pencil holders, etc.;
4. have difficulty shifting from one task to another;
5. notice every distraction in the classroom — become a self-appointed reporter of flickering lights, hornets, changes in the weather, aromas from the lunch room, etc.;
6. seem unable to work independently;
7. function best under a rigid schedule;
8. be the last one chosen for team games and sports;
9. have difficulty following directions and frequently ask to have directions repeated;
10. be unable to remember the multiplication and/or division tables;
11. make a short story long — his or her skills as a storyteller delay having to get down to work;
12. welcome all distractions from class work, such as a visit from the school nurse.

In General
A 10-year-old who is under an excessive amount of stress may:

1. become passive;
2. act defensively when reminded to finish work;
3. develop a nervous tic — a twitching eye, a nervous cough, frequent clearing of the throat or twirling hair;
4. fear being promoted to the next grade;
5. seem depressed.

Note: All children display some stress signs at times. Severe stress is indicated when a child consistently displays several stress signs over an extended period of time.

11-Year-Olds: Signs and signals of school stress

At School

An 11–year–old suffering from school-related stress may:

1. prefer to play with younger children;
2. try to avoid cursive writing and ask permission to print (or try to negotiate: "If I write the first five sentences cursively, can I print the next five?");
3. prefer using crayons instead of colored pencils, because crayons are easier to hold and use;
4. toy with such items as pencils, fancy erasers, and scissors (he may discover that he can dismantle his pen and make it into a whistle);
5. prefer white paper instead of yellow, because yellow tears more easily when she erases (which is constantly);
6. want continual reassurance and checking of work ("Is this right?");
7. choose individual rather than team sports;
8. find many excuses for moving around the class-room — such as watering the plants — when it's time to write;
9. frequently forget to bring in permission slips, absentee notes, lunch, musical instruments, etc.;
10. write very brief reports;
11. seldom if ever volunteer;
12. become the self-appointed class timekeeper ("Ten more minutes until recess!");
13. make excuses for work, such as claims that "I was never taught that in fifth grade."
14. have a difficult time writing a report in his/her own words;
15. produce challenging school work only when under constant pressure from parents and teacher;
16. prefer "concrete" subjects and have difficulty understanding abstractions, such as concepts and relationships or cause and effect.

In General
An 11–year–old who is under excessive stress at school
may:

1. fear being promoted to the next grade;
2. develop imaginary illnesses and injuries, such as a
   limp, bump, various aches, etc.;
3. have a poor self-image and low self-esteem;
4. write very small or very large;
5. compare himself or herself negatively to other
   students;
6. seem depressed;
7. talk about running away.

Note: All children display some stress signs at times.
Severe stress is indicated when a child consistently
displays several stress signs over an extended period of
time.

Middle School/Junior High School:
Signs and signals of school stress

At School

A student experiencing the stress of being in the wrong grade or program may:

1. want to visit his or her previous grade;
2. fall way behind with homework;
3. act like a clown in class;
4. complain that there is no recess;
5. be confused about the daily schedule, and about changing classes and teachers;
6. have school notebooks that are nearly blank inside;
7. become obsessed with a fear of going on to senior high school;
8. drop the study of a musical instrument because of loss of interest;
9. participate only passively in school activities — not become involved with plays, the yearbook, dances, contests, or any other extracurricular activities;
10. focus exclusively on academics — seem unable to handle involvement both in school life and social life;
11. have difficulty coping with departmentalization;
12. display immature behavior at dances or while viewing some life education films/videos;
13. be promoted to senior high school on trial;
14. begin to "act out" while riding on the school bus.

In General

A pre-adolescent student who is under excessive stress at school may:

1. procrastinate and/or manage time poorly;
2. complain about nearly everything — school, the teacher, the school building, the other kids, life in general;
3. lack motivation;
4. begin to have discipline problems;
5. play with younger children after school, on weekends, and during vacations;
6. refuse to take direction from parents, yet be unable to make own choices;
7. talk about suicide;
8. exhibit an eating disorder;
9. feel inferior;
10. talk about running away;
11. begin to use alcohol or controlled substances.

Note: All pre-adolescents and adolescents display some stress signs at times. Severe stress is indicated when a student consistently displays several stress signs over an extended period of time.

Senior High School: signs and signals of school stress

At School

A student experiencing excessive stress in a senior high school program may:

1. have failing grades;
2. not complete homework assignments;
3. cause problems on the school bus in the afternoon — releasing tension built up during the day;
4. cut classes and/or skip school frequently;
5. refuse to make up work;
6. do only enough to meet minimal requirements;
7. not seek the extra help that's needed;
8. have difficulty adapting to the senior high school schedule;
9. produce work that does not reflect his or her innate ability;
10. take only easy subjects;
11. not participate in any extracurricular activities.

In General

An adolescent student who is under excessive stress at school may:

1. complain constantly;
2. use time unwisely;
3. develop discipline problems;
4. rely excessively on a mentor, such as a guidance counselor, nurse, or teacher;
5. talk about dropping out of school and getting a job;
6. become self-destructive — for example, start abusing alcohol or using controlled substances;
7. neglect to inform parents of important matters, such as the dates of the SAT's or the deadline for an important scholarship application;
8. begin to fight losing battles with authority figures;
9. fantasize about suicide;
10. exhibit an eating disorder;
11. feel inferior;
12. talk about running away.

Note: All adolescents display some stress signs at times. Severe stress is indicated when a student consistently displays several stress signs over an extended period of time.

College: Signs and signals of school stress

At College
A student experiencing excessive stress in college may:

1. receive poor grades;
2. complain that he or she can't study because the dorm is too noisy (or too quiet);
3. cut classes;
4. complain about all the courses and all the professors;
5. complain that college is "too easy" or "too boring;"
6. make self-destructive choices — for example, when it's time to study, he plays touch football, and then when the game's over, he goes out for a beer;
7. spend time only on academics, participating in no extracurricular collegiate activities;
8. never quite find a major;
9. last only one semester and then quit.

In General
A student under excessive stress at college may:

1. call home constantly or come home every weekend;
2. love to visit "my old high school" to keep "one foot in the high school camp;"
3. talk constantly of transferring to another college;
4. flirt with the idea of quitting college and working or taking time off for a year;
5. develop a strong interest in cults that offer a supportive, family-style environment;
6. fantasize about suicide;
7. exhibit an eating disorder;
8. feel inferior;
9. pull out his or her hair;
10. develop a dependence on alcohol or controlled substances.

Note: All college students display some stress signs at times. Severe stress is indicated when a student consistently displays several stress signs over an extended period of time.

CHAPTER 5

Readiness Is A Common-Sense Concept

"It would be a fallacy to think all children are ready at the same time. 'Late bloomers' deserve to be identified and have their pace respected."
- T. Berry Brazelton, M.D., *Touchpoints*

The America 2000 education proposals include a plan to help the nation increase the readiness of its students through improved pre-natal and post-natal care, proper nutrition, and wider access to Head Start and pre-school programs. These are vital steps that can do much to determine whether a child initially experiences school success or — heaven forbid — school failure.

However, there is another crucial factor that strongly influences a child's initial educational experience, and it cannot be improved, sped up, or changed in any significant way. That is the child's individual rate and process of development, which determines the child's current developmental stage.

What does "developmental stage" mean?

A child's developmental stage refers to the level at which the child is functioning as a total human being, including his or her hands, eyes, muscles, bones, nervous system, and brain. A school-age child at a particular stage of development can perform certain tasks with skill and ease, while the same child will not be able to do certain other things well until further biological development occurs.

Unfortunately, a child's developmental stage may not correspond exactly with his or her chronological age.

Children go through predictable stages of development which are similar for every healthy, normal child, but the timing of these stages can vary widely. In fact, many experts believe that a child can be as much as a year ahead or behind the chronological average, and still be considered normal. These variations are compounded by schools' reliance on entrance cut-off dates, which result in some children being much younger chronologically than others in their class, as well as developmentally young.

Most parents recognize that every child does not reach the same level of development at exactly the same age as every other child. And, most parents also recognize the futility of trying to control variations in development. You cannot simply tell a child, "Okay, Johnny, Sam started walking when he was 1-year-old. Today you turned 1, so start walking." Of course, a parent can try this approach, but what happens next is probably a better lesson for the parent than the child. Life simply does not work this way.

Variations in development continue throughout the early childhood years. Jean may begin talking at 11 months and Janet at 21 months, and both are developing their speaking abilities within a normal, perfectly acceptable time span for children. Both are perfectly okay and doing exactly what they should be doing.

Virtually all of a young child's initial achievements occur in this way. Children crawl when they are ready. They teethe when they are ready. They walk when they are ready. They talk when they are ready. But, somehow, they are all expected to be ready for the same educational experience at the same time, and expected to complete it in the same amount of time.

Development is not a contest

The reality is that a child who talks at an early age is not superior to a child who talks several months later. When it comes to sending their children to school, however, parents sometimes ignore what their own sense and experience tell them. On one level, they may realize that Matt or Susie or Steve or Sally would benefit from extra time to develop, or from participating in a program better matched to their current stage of development. Yet, some parents may still end up denying the evidence before their eyes, not trusting their own judgement because of others' opinions or because they think proceeding at a slower pace will somehow put their child at a competitive disadvantage. In fact, the child at a competitive disadvantage is the one who is developmentally too young for a particular grade or program, rather than one who takes the time needed to develop and succeed.

...parents may still end up denying the evidence before their eyes...

First grade, for example, requires a child to have the ability to concentrate despite distractions and to cope with a full day at school. First grade also requires coordination between the hands and eyes, so that a child can write words on a page. A child who has not reached the developmental stage needed to meet these requirements is at risk and may fail first grade, no matter how smart that child is.

While much has been done to make the primary grades more developmentally appropriate for young children, there remain strong pressures to increase the amount of formal academic instruction. In addition to the pressures created by politicians and some educators, pressure may also come from parents who think that speeding up a child's intellectual development is advantageous, and that other aspects of development are far less important.

The whole child goes to school

If you listen to some educators and some parents, you might think that intelligence is the one and only key to school success. Simply stuffing a young child's head with words and numbers, and providing extensive computer training, might seem like the sole responsibility of a school.

"Too many parents — and teachers — get great pleasure from watching a 4-year-old count to 50. But what good does that do when the child has no concept of what 50 is? Even a parrot can mimic numbers."
- Harold Jaus, Associate Professor of Education at Purdue University, quoted in *The New York Times*

For better or worse, young children are not computers which can be fed information that is stored, processed, and then spit out in different ways. When young children learn a subject by rote, they do not understand the information and cannot apply it to other areas of their lives. The real lesson they have learned under these circumstances is how to please adults.

Children are complete human beings — not memory storage units — and they need to develop their physical, social, and emotional capabilities, as well as their intellectual capabilities. As noted earlier, attempts to speed up and overemphasize intellectual development not only fail to educate a child effectively, they may backfire and actually lead to poor performance in school. Even if successful, such efforts can also result in a child who is developmentally out of balance — a child in danger of becoming, unhappily, the class "bookworm" or "brain."

This can be a particularly difficult problem because a child does not necessarily mature in all areas of development at the same rate. It is not unusual, for example, to see a child function at the level of a 7-year-old intellectually, but when the child's physical, social, and emotional capabilities are factored in, the overall developmental stage is more like that of a 5-year-old.

...consider all four aspects of development...

A common-sense approach to readiness therefore requires adults to consider all four aspects of development when determining a child's placement in a specific grade or program. The following sections look in more detail at the importance of three aspects of readiness other than intellect.

Happiness is having a friend

When young children are going to school for the very first time, what do you think their primary concern is? If you think they are worrying only about learning to read and write, or any other academic matter, think again.

Having or not having a friend is extremely important, which is natural when you consider that these young children are going to be separated from their parents and any other personal caregiver for a set period of time every day. Their standing with their peer group is much more significant than it was in the past, which is why the social aspects of a child's developmental stage are a very important consideration when considering placement in a grade or program.

A parent who has had to watch while his or her child was chosen last will know just how painful school can be for a child too young to fit in. And, while pre-school experience and parental "coaching" can help with some aspects of a child's social development, a child at a younger developmental stage will still be well aware of the difference, as will the child's peers. The primary grades are an important period in the development of a child's self-image, so frequent feelings of rejection or inferiority can have serious and long-lasting consequences.

Breaking up me and mom

Is the child emotionally ready for school? Can she really share "my" teacher with all the other kids? Will he be traumatized riding on the school bus with those fourth grade giants who are saying "the big swears?" Can each child handle stressful classroom demands?

Some children become upset when another child is scolded, as if being in trouble is instantly contagious. When the little girl comes home from school with her bottom lip curled and quivering, and Mom picks up the body language and asks, "What happened?", Sally might answer, "Matt got scolded today. Matt was sitting just two seats away from me. Maybe next time she'll come over and scold me."

Can the child stand the separation from home? Imagine the fortunate child who usually had lunch with Mom at home prior to starting to school. The child remembers, "Mom always had soup and a sandwich for me. Every day at twelve o'clock, Mom and I had time together. And, she never made me eat anything I don't like. Now, I go to school and I'm not served first; I'm served sixty-first. I stand in line with my plate, and every step I take brings me closer to the hot lunch lady. Under my breath, I'm rehearsing what I'll say to her: 'No, thank you. I don't care for any.' And, finally I am standing in front of the hot lunch lady, who seems like she was born with a scoop arm. And, I say out loud, 'No, thank you,' and she says, 'What? Of course, you'll eat it! Your parents paid good money in taxes, and the government gave this to us to eat. You can't waste good food like this, not when there are children starving.' 'But I'll throw up,' I whisper. And then the hot lunch lady's voice might just soften and say, 'Okay, today you can give it back.'"

Many children are scared sick, literally...

Many children are scared sick, literally, because emotionally they are just too young for school.

When it's okay to play hooky

The physical strain young children experience in school is considerable. If you can remember what it was like to learn to read (few people can), or if you have recently watched a child go through this process, you will know that it takes tremendous energy to concentrate mind, body, and soul on a twenty-minute reading lesson. And, watch the contortions a first grader goes through when learning to write. He may squeeze his pencil so tightly that his fingertips turn white; his neck and shoulder muscles may become visibly tense and tight. The girl sitting next to him may have her tongue sticking out of her mouth and moving, helping the writing process along.

Learning to write involves the entire child in a very difficult task of coordinating mind and muscles in a way never done before. After fifteen or twenty minutes, the child is usually exhausted. And, after a five-and-a-quarter-hour day in school, many children urgently need a nap.

For some young children, school pressures cause illness. It is no coincidence that first grade tends to be the grade with the highest rate of absenteeism. When my wife and I used to sense that one of our children was overly strained and tired, we would let him take a "health break" — a day off from school during which he could stay relaxed in his pajamas until noon. Playing "hooky" once in a while with parents' permission can give some children the break they need to proceed successfully through the school year. But, other children need much more time before the school year even begins, in order to reach the developmental stage at which they can succeed.

How do you measure a child's readiness?

Do you have concerns about a child's readiness for a particular grade or program? How can you identify the right grade or program for the child's developmental stage? How can you help any child achieve success in school right from the beginning?

During the last few decades, as awareness of the importance of readiness has increased, educators and other experts on early childhood have used evaluation tools known as "developmental assessments" or "school readiness screening examinations" to provide information about a child's current stage of development. These evaluations measure such things as a child's motor skills, coordination, attention span, visual perception, clarity of speech, ability to follow directions, and ability to sustain a function — all important elements of school success in the primary grades.

There are no wrong answers in this sort of evaluation, as it simply helps to identify the child's current stage of development so that an appropriate program placement decision can be made. It is also quite different from an I.Q. test or reading readiness test, which do not provide information about a child's overall developmental level. Most children actually enjoy participating in a developmental assessment, because it uses age-appropriate techniques and focuses on what a child can do.

These sorts of evaluations are based on extensive research which includes long and careful observation of thousands of children of various ages. The best known and most popular are the Gesell Developmental Assessments, which grew out of the work of Dr. Arnold Gesell, a professor at Yale University who devoted much of his work to the study of child development. Most other evaluation tools of this sort are patterned after the Gesell Assessments and borrow from Dr. Gesell's pioneering research.

When making placement decisions, the information provided by a developmental assessment or school readiness screening should always be combined with other information based on parents' and teachers' observations. Parents can provide important information about a child's prior development, which can help explain and confirm evaluation results. Teachers can utilize their years of experience observing children in group situations, as well as their firsthand knowledge of whatever educational programs are available. Through the use of all this information, parents and educators working together can make the best possible decisions for the children in their care.

"As decisions about preschool, kindergarten, and first grade arise, the following reasons to give children extra time should be considered:

Family patterns of slow development — "late bloomers"
Prematurity or physical problems in early life
Immature motor development — awkwardness, poor motor skills,

such as in catching or throwing a ball, drawing, or cutting
Easy distractibility and short attention span
Difficulty with right-left hand or eye-hand coordination, such as in
copying a circle or diamond
Lagging social development — difficulty taking turns, sharing, or
playing. If the child is shunned by children her own age, take it
seriously.

Each of these might be a reason to allow a child to mature another
year before starting preschool, or to stay in preschool or kindergarten
a year longer."
- T. Berry Brazelton, M.D., *Touchpoints*

How to recognize a developmental assessment or school readiness screening examination when you see one

It is important to remember that not every screening instrument used to evaluate children developmentally is readiness-oriented. Schools screen and test children for a variety of reasons, such as trying to determine specific abilities or identify children who are considered "culturally disadvantaged," "educationally handicapped," "gifted," etc. An instrument designed for these purposes is fundamentally different from a developmental readiness screening examination.

The following checklist will help you to understand and recognize effective school readiness screening examinations:

Readiness Evaluation Checklist
Eleven Vital Characteristics of an
Effective School Readiness Screening Examination

1. The examination is individually administered.
2. The examiner has achieved a required professional standard of training.
3. The examination measures the "whole" child, including the emotional, social, physical, and intellectual aspects of development.

4. The examination is not culturally, linguistically, or economically biased.
5. The examination is not weighted heavily on language development.
6. The examination has proven to be valid and reliable, based on research compiled by the school or other education organization.
7. The examination follows a stated philosophical point of view based on established principles of child development.
8. The process by which a child completes a task is as important or more important than the task itself.
9. All answers are correct for the respondent.
10. No child ever "fails."
11. The examination provides a score or range designed to be used for a program or grade recommendation, and to match the curriculum to the child.

Readiness for what?

...every child is ready for some sort of learning experience...

When working with developmental readiness evaluation results, the most important question is not *whether* a child is ready for *one* particular grade or program; instead the key question is *which* grade or program the child is ready for. Responsible educators recognize that every child is ready for some sort of learning experience, and that schools should provide options that meet different children's needs. With this approach in mind, developmental readiness evaluations help to ensure that schools are ready for their students, rather than forcing students to be ready for the same "one-size-fits-all" curriculum.

Whoever coined the phrase, "nothing succeeds like success," had a good understanding of how children — and adults, for that matter — achieve. Success creates the confidence and positive attitudes that lead to more success. When young children are provided with educational experiences for which they are ready, they succeed in learning and then are intellectually and emotionally ready for a new learning experience.

These children become students who learn well and enjoy learning.

In contrast, consider the plight of a late bloomer who struggles through initial school experiences which are *not* developmentally appropriate for the child. Intellectually, this child has not mastered the concepts needed for the next stage of the learning process. Emotionally, this child is likely to have negative expectations, based on both previous experience and the recognition that the solid base of knowledge needed for new learning experiences is lacking. Until a situation like this is put right, a child is increasingly likely to end up saying "I hate school!"

This is the sort of result that developmental readiness evaluations and extra-time options are designed to avoid. In the next chapter, we'll explore some of the successful options that schools now provide to help students achieve the success they deserve.

CH

T

T

"...   le is
lik   too
m   have
p   ears,
a   "

967,
com–
acher
ieved
year,
to see
nd we
d mo–
Temple

"Well," I said, "I may not ...   ut I am gifted in math, and I know that would make me Temple's fifth principal in twenty-four months. I'm not sure I can stand that kind of upward mobility." In spite of my reservations, when I woke up the following Monday, I was the principal of an elementary school.

The teacher of the first/second multi-age classroom presented me with my first challenge. "I don't know what I'm going to do with my twenty-five children," she said. "They're all over the place. I have trouble getting them to slow down long enough for me to teach them."

I went to her classroom, opened the door, and quickly closed it. Nothing in my teacher education classes or one year of actual teaching experience had prepared me to deal with what I saw.

It was then that I brought in my former teacher, Nancy Richard, as an early childhood consultant who could advise me on the children's development. She observed the class and said, "You have second graders doing third grade work, second graders doing second grade work, second graders doing first grade work, first graders doing second grade work, first graders doing first grade work, first graders doing no work at all, and then there are two boys in the corner who aren't toilet trained after lunch."

"Some of these children," she continued, "aren't yet ready to do first grade work. Chronologically, they are 6, but developmentally they are still too young to succeed in that class." She then suggested that I take a course on "developmental readiness."

In that course, I was surprised to learn that up to twenty-five percent of the children in American schools repeat a grade, and as many as another twenty-five percent are often struggling and not succeeding in their current grade. I checked the registers covering a six-year period at my school and proved those statistics were flawed. In my school, thirty-three percent of the kids had repeated! This informal survey also showed that most of the children who repeated were boys, and the grade most children repeated was first grade.

Being a bright, young, "overplaced" principal, I immediately made two brilliant deductions: boys are stupid, and first grade teachers are incompetent. Further reflection, observation, and discussion led me to some different conclusions, however. I began to consider the possibility that girls tended to develop more rapidly in certain respects than boys, and that these differences reached the crisis point in first grade, when all the children were expected to learn how to read and write.

One September in the late 1960's, we began to screen children to help determine their developmental readiness for a first grade experience. We discovered that many of the children eligible for first grade on the basis of their age that year were at risk for a traditional first grade program. When I shared that news with their parents and recommended that the developmentally young children remain in kindergarten for another year, the parents were very unhappy. They decided to send all of those late-blooming children into first grade together, thinking that the children being together would somehow make a difference in their developmental readiness for the demands of first grade.

Of course, it did not. By the middle of October, several of the children had been withdrawn from first grade at their parents' request and moved back to kindergarten. The problems that were surfacing at home and at school made the parents realize that these children really did need more time to grow and prepare for first grade. The rest of the developmentally young children ended up taking two years to complete first grade.

...these children really did need more time to grow...

The next year, when we assessed the entering children's developmental levels, we did more to inform the parents — at PTA meetings, in one-on-one meetings, through literature. That year, many children who were developmentally young stayed in kindergarten for an extra year, and then entered first grade when most were 7-years-old. That first group of children, who had the advantage of an extra year to grow, graduated from high school in 1982, and many went on to graduate from college in 1986. We've been using this developmental approach in schools across New Hampshire for well over two decades — with success.

Nationwide, thousands of schools also began providing developmentally young children with extra-time options during the 1960's, helping tens of thousands of students master the curriculum and achieve success in school. This concept, which was formulated in 1911 and formalized as a Title III government program in New Hampshire in 1966, spread rapidly as teachers and parents recognized firsthand how much some children benefited from having an extra year to develop, which then gave them a much greater chance to succeed in school.

Now, when many parents and politicians are demanding stricter standards and measurements of progress, at the same time that many young children are feeling the effects of the disintegration of families and communities, there is a greater need than ever to provide extra-time options for children who are developmentally too young to succeed in a particular grade or program.

The wrong way — vs. the right way — to learn

"I would contend that much of today's school failure results from academic expectations for which students' brains were not prepared — but which were bulldozed into them anyway."
- Jane M. Healy, Ph.D., *Endangered Minds*

One kindergarten teacher told me this story:

"When parents in my school district demanded that kindergarten children be taught reading, a formal first grade reading program was introduced into the half-day kindergarten. Naturally, most of the children could not cope with this program. The school board decided that the half-day time constraint was the reason the program didn't work. So, they extended kindergarten to a full day, but most 5-year-olds still had problems with the reading program, and now they had an additional problem: many could not handle a full day of school that included this sort of work. The school board then appointed a study committee to investigate the merits of implementing a mandatory program for 4-year-olds. In other words, rather than providing developmentally appropriate work for each age level, the push for early reading started turning preschool and kindergarten into prep schools for first grade!"

...most of the children could not cope with this program.

Some people still think an early start in academics gives children an advantage, rather than creating frustration and negative attitudes. However, many educators and parents have learned the hard way that an overly academic approach in the primary grades requires teaching in ways that are out of sync with the needs of young children. The result is an early lesson in how to achieve failure.

In the primary grades, children need learning experiences that are direct and hands-on, because they are not capable of understanding abstract concepts until they are older. When taught math and science using objects they can actually feel, move, and see, young children learn far better than when they are asked to work only with abstract symbols such as words and numerals.

Children also benefit when they learn to read using colorful, interesting, and varied books, rather than just the "basal readers" known for their limited subject matter and limited appeal. When learning to write, children gain knowledge and confidence by going through a "publishing" process that includes editing and correcting their work, then sharing it with others by reading it aloud. This process allows them to use "invented" or "temporary" spelling initially, so as not to detract from their desire to learn or from their confidence, but it also encourages them to learn correct spelling in an appropriate, supportive way. Together, these widely used "whole language" strategies to teach reading and writing are an integral part of developmentally appropriate education.

Other popular developmental teaching techniques include the use of "themes" to integrate different subjects through the exploration of multi-faceted topics; and the use of "learning centers," where children can work together on specific projects or subjects, rather than having to sit at the same desk all day and listen while the teacher talks. Vast numbers of primary grade teachers now use combinations of techniques such as these, making classrooms across America more educational, developmentally appropriate, and enjoyable for students.

However, some educational theorists now go so far as to claim that the use of these innovative techniques eliminates the need for extra-time options. Once schools have a "developmentally appropriate" curriculum, the theory goes, variations in development and learning rates will even out by the time the children reach third grade. And, until children reach this wonderful stage, classroom teachers can simply individualize the curriculum so that not a single child — anywhere in the United States — will ever fail or need extra time to master the curriculum during the vital early years of school.

Unfortunately, the proponents of this theory (mostly university professors, along with some administrators) have failed for years to identify a single school where this is actually occurring. And, third grade teachers at schools which do use a developmental approach tend to break into either laughter or tears when told that all the children in their classes should now be catching up with each other and learning successfully. The theory has therefore been revised by some to say that all the children will catch up in fourth grade (this has been called "developmental inflation"), but most fourth grade teachers will advise you not to try holding your breath until this happens, either.

Curriculum and time are two separate issues

In fact, there is no "magic" curriculum or grouping of children which will eliminate the need for young children to develop at different rates. A 6-year-old child who is developmentally too young to read will be unable to comprehend how our written language works in even the most interesting, colorful children's book. But, given an extra year to grow in a supportive, educational environment, the same child is usually ready and able to learn to read. This has been shown to be true in schools across America and is also just plain common sense — something noticeably lacking in a number of education theories.

The hard realities facing today's students, parents and teachers make extra-time options even more necessary — not less necessary — than they have been in the past. As noted earlier, budget constraints in many school districts have resulted in larger class sizes and limited availability of materials, preventing many teachers from providing the individualized, develop- *...many* mentally appropriate curriculum they would like their *students are* students to have. And, many students are now starting *now starting* school less prepared to learn than in previous decades, *school less* due to problems ranging from outright hunger to the *prepared to* complex effects of being raised in a dysfunctional fam- *learn...* ily. This trend has been further complicated by the "full inclusion" of severely handicapped children who formerly would have been in separate special education classes, and who now require extra attention from classroom teachers who often have not been trained to work effectively with "differently-able" children.

At the same time, parents and politicians who demand a more academic curriculum and stricter standards have succeeded in increasing the pressure on many students, who now must demonstrate certain capabilities in a set period of time in order to "make the grade," or suffer the consequences. To top it all off, many teachers are also being told they should not retain any children for a second year in the same grade, or provide any other form of additional learning time, due to the costs involved.

If most of today's students were coming to school well-fed, well-rested, and well-prepared to learn, as in the past, the effects of these pressures might be less severe. Unfortunately, study after study has shown that too many of today's students are coming to school hungry, tired, stressed, and ill-prepared to meet the standards being imposed on them, even in relatively affluent areas. And, when many of the same students are also emotionally needy due to problems within their families and communities, the classroom becomes even less conducive to learning, and the teacher must spend even more time being a social worker rather than an educator.

Under these circumstances, a refusal to provide time-flexibility options often sets up the students and teachers for failure. Developmentally young children who are struggling in an inappropriate grade or program need extensive help just to get by, and they are very unlikely to receive it when so many children are in need and teachers are so over-burdened. By the end of the school year, these children's self-esteem has usually been eroded, their mastery of the subject matter is limited at best, and their attitudes towards school and the people in their lives are increasingly negative. Then, if they must be "socially promoted" into the next grade, they go through the same cycle all over again, falling even further behind, doubting themselves even more, and becoming all the more likely to say, "I hate school!"

Extra time in a supportive environment helps these children...

Fortunately, many schools offer time-flexibility options that allow developmentally young children to become the successful late-bloomers they can and should be. Extra time in a supportive environment helps these children develop the intellectual, physical, social and emotional capabilities to meet the demands of an appropriate grade or program, so they become confident learners who can stay at the top of the class — rather than the bottom.

"When children face a school environment that is too sophisticated and busy for their current stage of development, they start to see themselves as being incapable of doing anything right. This is where the pattern of failure begins, and it may never go away."
- Judy Keshner, *Starting School*

Time-flexibility options

Programs that provide children with an extra year of growing time have many different names, but they share a number of common features. A good time-flexibility program offers reasonable class sizes, an environment rich in materials, and a room with space for movement. Here children can develop their physical and motor capabilities, learn social skills, work with hands-on math and science materials, practice listening and speaking, gain experience with different types of literature, explore the creative arts, and develop problem-solving abilities. As a result, children in these programs can develop the habits of success and a positive attitude toward school.

These programs emphasize an interest-based approach to learning rather than a curriculum based on text books and "time on task," access to a wide variety of literature instead of just basal readers and workbooks, and the use of authentic assessments rather than standardized achievement tests. All of these characteristics should be found in any of the time-flexibility options described below:

Readiness classes for "Young 5's"

Many schools continue to find that a large number of entering students are developmentally too young to learn and succeed in kindergarten. This may be due to a child's innate but still normal rate of development, or environmental factors which have left a child unprepared to work well in a kindergarten class. Readiness classes provide the time needed to grow and make the transition to the school environment in a supportive setting, which then makes kindergarten a much more positive and educational experience. This is particularly important because, as kindergarten teacher Judy Keshner explains in her booklet, *Starting School*, kindergarten "is not a preview of what is to come — it is the foundation on which the following years will grow. Each grade builds on the one that came before, and kindergarten sets the pattern and the tone."

Developmental "two-tier" kindergarten

In this type of program, all 5-year-olds enter kindergarten at the same time, based on the legal entrance age, but some stay for one year and some stay for two. After enrollment, each child is developmentally assessed and continues to be observed throughout the year, so that detailed information about children's rate and stage of development is available. At the end of the school year, those children who are developmentally ready move on to first grade. Children who need more time to develop in order to enhance their experience in first grade can remain in kindergarten for a second year, or move into the sort of pre-first or transition class described below.

Pre-first grade, transition grade, bridge classes

Call it what you will, this sort of extra-year option has been adopted by concerned parents, teachers, and administrators across America. It provides developmentally young 6-year-olds with a continuous-progress, full-day program in which they have extra time to grow and learn. This helps them make the very difficult and important transition from the play-oriented learning of kindergarten to the more formal "academic tasks" which become increasingly important in first grade. Developmentally young children who have had this extra-year experience are then much better prepared to enter first grade with confidence and a reasonable expectation of success.

Readiness/First Grade (R/1) Configuration

This approach acknowledges the reality that continues to exist in most first grade classes: children who need extra time to grow are blended with those who are developmentally ready for first grade. What makes the R/1 configuration different is that the parents of children who need extra time know from the very beginning that their children can have two years to complete this blended first grade, if needed. This takes the pressure off everyone — students, teachers, and mom and dad. There are no high-stakes campaigns to pass "or else," and no end-of-the-year trauma for children who just need more time to grow and develop.

Some schools choose the R/1 configuration to save money — by not having a separate readiness class, they save on classroom space, staffing, and materials. Other schools choose this option because it is the one the educators prefer and the community accepts. It also provides the many benefits of the multi-age classes described below, such as allowing developmentally young students to work closely with and learn from more experienced students during their first year, and then to become the models for new students during their second year.

Multi-age primary classes

An increasing number of schools now offer multi-age primary classrooms, in which children of different ages work and learn together, staying together with the teacher for a multi-year placement. These classrooms eliminate the artificial time constraints created by having separate grades from kindergarten through third grade.

One important result is that more time is available for teaching and learning, especially at the start of the year, as teachers and students don't have to spend time getting to know one another and learning to work well together. This approach also eliminates worries about "running out of time" to complete the curriculum by the end of each year, and it eliminates many high-stakes decisions which otherwise have to be made each year. In addition, if a child needs extra time to develop and complete the curriculum before moving on, a multi-age class works particularly well because it already contains a wide range of age levels and a flexible timetable, rather than a rigid, lock-step grade structure.

...more time is available for teaching and learning...

Multi-age classrooms decrease the risk of failure for all children, because these classes allow students to develop and learn at their own rate in a much less hurried environment. Staying in the same class with the same teacher and classmates for more than one year also provides a sense of consistency and belonging, which can be particularly helpful for the many children who now grow up in fast-changing families and communities. And, the developmental diversity that naturally occurs in a multi-age classroom makes it easier for transfer and special-needs students to be included in them.

An extra year of preschool

Unfortunately, too many parents have to cope with schools which do not offer viable extra-time options for children who are developmentally too young to succeed in kindergarten. Under these circumstances, allowing developmentally young children to spend an extra year in preschool can be a very positive alternative to sending them off to kindergarten and waiting to find out if they "sink or swim." Having an extra year to grow and learn in a supportive preschool environment greatly decreases the odds that such children will flounder and need rescuing in the primary grades.

High-quality preschools provide children with a range of developmentally appropriate activities that foster continued growth and learning. And, the mixed age levels found in most preschools makes it easy for developmentally young children to fit in, just as in a multiage class. This sort of environment also tends to make preschool teachers aware of the importance of readiness and adept at working with children who are at various developmental levels. Unfortunately, in most cases this option is only available to financially advantaged parents.

An extra year at home

Some parents may prefer to provide their late bloomer with day care and learning experiences at home for an extra year. In situations where there is a parent at home every day who has the time, inclination, and understanding to work with a child in this way, it can be a viable alternative, especially now that more materials and support networks have been developed for the small but growing number of parents who opt to provide their children's entire education at home.

In many cases, parents can simply notify the local school of their intent and send children to kindergarten when they are 6-years-old. However, young children need opportunities to grow and learn with their peers, which contribute in many ways to a child's overall development. And, well-trained preschool and elementary school teachers can often provide a wider range of supportive and educational learning experiences for a developmentally young child than a parent.

...young children need opportunities to grow and learn with their peers...

Dropping out and "stopping out"

When developmentally young children do not take extra time early in their educational career, they tend to take the time later on. They may repeat a grade in middle school or high school, or flunk out or drop out altogether. They may also obtain their high school diploma but feel the need to take time off before going to college. Some "stop out" — a phrase used to describe students who take a leave of absence while at college. Statistics show that a large number of students do take time off during college, and interestingly enough, the percentage is about the same as the percentage of children found to need extra time when they start school!

Some young people may be ready to put the extra time to better use when they are older, but too many end up with negative attitudes, low self-esteem, and poor skills that interfere with their ability to create productive and fulfilling lives. Early intervention in a positive and supportive way can be far more effective than a wait-and-see approach.

Another year in the same grade

This important option warrants its own chapter, which immediately follows this one.

CHAPTER 7
Is It Okay To Correct A Mistake?

re·place (ree-plays) *verb* To allow a child to take two years of time in one grade in order to achieve a correct grade placement in school; traditionally known as retaining, repeating a grade, being left back, etc.

Matching a child to the correct grade or program in school is the most important decision adults make about the child's education. If a child is currently in the wrong grade or program, adults have a responsibility to correct that mistake, so that a long-lasting, positive change in the child's education occurs.

If you believe — or have a pretty strong hunch — that a child is now one grade ahead of where he or she should be, you have already taken a giant step toward solving the problem. Having identified the reason that the child is struggling in school, you can now find the solution.

If you determine that a child is overplaced in school, and other extra-time options are unavailable or inappropriate, replace the child. (By that, I don't mean you should go out and get a new child; I mean that you should give the child a chance to make a new beginning in the grade or program appropriate for the child.)

"Oh, if only it were that easy!" Isn't that what you're thinking? "How can I be sure I'm not making a terrible mistake? Doesn't it damage self-esteem? Won't the other kids tease him? Won't he end up like the big kids in the back of the room — the ones who were just waiting to drop out when I was in school?"

These are troubling and serious questions, of course, but these same questions must also be asked about the risk of allowing the child to remain overplaced, so that his or her educational experience continues to be frustrating, negative, and unsuccessful. My answer, which is also the answer of many other experienced educators, is that I have seen numerous children become happy, confident, successful students once they have taken the two years they need to reach the developmental stage at which they can master the curriculum.

Replacement is not right for every child, but neither is tutoring or just doing nothing and hoping for the best. It is the responsibility of the parents and educators in a child's life to weigh the risks and advantages, and then make the decision that best meets the specific needs of that individual child.

"Some people fear that holding a child back will hurt his feelings and damage his ego...But what could be worse for his self-esteem than not being able to read or solve problems, and being at the bottom of the class?"
- Louise Bates Ames, Ph.D., in the April, 1994 issue of Parenting Magazine

Giving children a second chance at school success

Let me say right off that I am a firm believer in replacing students at any grade level or age, and at any time during the school year. I also believe that replacement can be achieved without harm to the child and without unusual stress. In fact, I have found, as have many other educators, that children often feel a great sense of relief when they are told they will be spending more time in a grade, because they know they won't have to keep trying to do the impossible.

While there are some ideological extremists who want to prohibit all children from ever spending two years in the same grade, grade replacement remains widespread in the United States, and the policies and procedures determining when and how it occurs vary widely. Some schools will not replace students unless a very assertive parent absolutely insists on it. In other schools, all that's required is the agreement of the parents and teacher; they notify the principal of their decision, so that he or she can revise the school register, and the deed is done.

The basis on which replacement decisions are made also varies widely. Some schools rely solely on standardized achievement test scores, which measure only the cognitive area of development. More enlightened schools consider a variety of other factors as well, including the child's emotional, social, and physical maturity; the child's birth date; I.Q. test scores; the attitude of the child and the child's parents; and, because girls tend to develop more rapidly than boys, the sex of the child.

To provide guidance to educators and parents, the National Association of Elementary School Principals has issued the following statement regarding replacement decisions:

"Children who do not keep exact pace are not labeled failures; a vigorous effort is made to learn why that child seems to be laggard and to correct the situation.

"If retention is considered, the decision is never based on a single factor but on a wide variety of considerations, using various assessment techniques and instruments and including observations by the principal, the teacher, the support staff, and parents."
- Early Childhood Education and the Elementary School Principal

Once the decision to replace a child has been made, two key factors determine whether the child has a positive or negative reaction to this important event — how the child is told about it, and any other clue the child picks up from parents and teachers.

The wrong way to tell a child about replacement

...children felt they were being punished...

Research shows that when many older children repeat a grade, their self-esteem is damaged. Along with everything else I believe, I believe these research findings are true. Why? Because they are often based on cases in which children felt they were being punished when they had to repeat a grade.

For example, suppose parents say to a child, "You know we have struggled with you for four years. Here you are now in fifth grade, and again you're barely making it. If you don't straighten yourself out, you're going to have to repeat fifth grade."

After this "wonderful heart-to-heart" talk, suppose the child is still unable to meet the requirements for this grade level. Then, he is told he is going to be left back. If this child is not hurt by this experience, he is a remarkable child who is not going to be hurt by anything done to him in school. The great majority of children in this situation, however, are going to believe there is something wrong with them, are going to blame themselves for failing, and are going to feel stupid.

Another way of handling the situation is a more gently worded message from the school and parents that would go something like this: "We know you have had a difficult time in school for five long years. We have tried to help you in a variety of ways, but for some reason the problems are continuing. We cannot in good conscience pass you on to the next grade. We want you to stay back in fifth grade this year, so you can get back on track. We're sure you will do better in school and be more comfortable next year."

Do you know what the child receiving this message actually thinks and feels?

"You are keeping me back because you think I am stupid! I tried my best, but it wasn't good enough for you. I already did fifth grade; you shouldn't have to make me do it again. Deep down, you think I don't try hard enough. Well, I do. I work just as hard as the other kids, maybe even harder. But, the other kids always seem to know more than I do, and I don't understand everything that's being taught. The teacher teaches too fast, and I don't have enough time to get things right.

"No matter how hard I work, it's never good enough for you people. I feel like I've been disappointing you ever since I started school. Now, you're going to leave me back, and let the whole world know that you think I'm stupid. You know how that makes me feel? It makes me feel so stupid and bad that I hate school, and I never want to go back."

Believe me when I tell you that a child does not — repeat *not* — have to feel badly about spending an extra year in the same grade. In fact, a child can feel very good about repeating a grade, and very good about himself because he has the opportunity to do it. Consider these comments from some actual repeaters:

"I know the answers this year. I love feeling that now I am one of the smartest kids in the class."

"The teacher doesn't have to nag me any more."

"For once, I am the one who can help the other kids. I'm not the one who always needs help."

"Now I have many friends in school."

"This is the first time since I started school that I can do what is expected of me."

What makes the difference between these responses and those described earlier in this section? Obviously, the actual experience has a lot to do with it, but so does the way in which it is presented.

The right way to tell your child about replacement: "Mom and Dad made a mistake."

In talking with a child about spending extra time in a grade, it is imperative to include three key elements in the conversation, if you want the child to feel good about remaining in the grade:

1. Make it abundantly clear to your child that you, the parents, made a mistake. You unknowingly allowed your child to be placed in the wrong grade or program, one for which he or she was not ready.

2. Enlist your child's aid in correcting this unfortunate mistake; ask the child to help set things right.

3. Make certain that there is agreement among parents, teacher, and principal that it is in the child's best interest to spend two years in the same grade. And, make sure the child understands that he or she has the whole-hearted support of all these adults.

I would suggest that when parents sit down to talk to a child about spending more time in the same grade, they say something like this:

"Son, I know that school has not been easy for you, this year and in the past. Recently, Mom and Dad attended a parents' meeting at the school, and we heard some new ideas and information which made us think again about some of the earlier decisions we made. After talking it over, we now realize why school is so difficult for you, and why the problem is our fault, not yours.

"For all these years, you've been assigned to the wrong grade. When you started going to school, you really weren't ready for the work in kindergarten, because you were too young. We sent you there because that's what we thought we were supposed to do, but we were wrong. It wasn't your fault when you couldn't do the work; you just needed more time to grow.

"No wonder you sometimes felt that you couldn't keep up with the rest of the class, and that school was unfair. We used to blame the teachers and the school sometimes, and other times we wondered if we had failed you as parents. We certainly didn't mean to make you feel you were at fault, and now that we know what the problem really is, we can change the situation and you can start feeling better about school.

"We want you to help us correct our mistake. We'd like you to stay with Mrs. Smith for another year and take two years to finish fifth grade. This may be a little difficult at times. The other kids may make some un-kind remarks. You will be doing some things over again. But, we are sure the benefits will outweigh the problems, or we wouldn't ask you to help us by doing this.

"Now, you'll have time to learn all the material, so you'll have a solid understanding when you go on to sixth grade. We don't want you to go on struggling year after year, and we want you to have time for some fun after school and during vacations. The single most important thing we want is for you to be happy with your life. Please help us achieve this by agreeing to stay in fifth grade."

When the matter is outlined to the child in this man-ner, there's a good chance the child will feel the bur-den of guilt shift to the parents. And, what a relief it is to have somebody else carry the burden — to have the heavy weight of four years of failure taken off a 10-year-old's back. It is especially uplifting when the par-ents are the ones who do it. The child actually hears the parents say they are the "guilty parties;" the child is not to blame and has done nothing wrong.

...the child will feel the burden of guilt shift to the parents.

In addition, the child now knows the real reason why the work in school was so difficult. It's not because the child is stupid; it's not because the child didn't try. The problem was that the child needed some extra time to grow and develop, and now that the child can have that time, he or she will be able do the work well and succeed in school.

Soon after the parents have this talk with the child, there should be a meeting at which the parents, the child, and the child's teacher are all present. At this meeting, it is helpful for the teacher to say something like the following, while the parents are there listening:

"I am glad you are going to be back in the classroom with me next year, and I am sure it is the right decision. Looking back from where we are today, I think the school should have had you take an extra year in kindergarten or first grade the way Larry and Kristen did, but that's all in the past. The important thing is that now we can do something to make the future much better for you.

"I will explain to the class that we have decided you should spend two years in my class. I want you to be my special helper next year. And, you won't have to repeat the work you already understand; I will have new, challenging materials and activities for you. You will simply begin where you left off. I promise you won't be bored, and I think you'll be pleasantly surprised at how much fun school can be when you don't have to struggle so much of the time. By the time the year's over, you'll feel good about going on to sixth grade."

The child can then feel secure...

The child can then feel secure, knowing that his or her parents and teacher are in complete harmony regarding this crucial issue. And, presenting grade replacement in this positive way may give the child a sense of stability in regard to school for the very first time. The end result is much more likely to be the sort of change for the better described in the following section.

Three success stories

Peter: Youngest child in class

"As he stood in the doorway of my classroom, he looked so young and frail. Twenty minutes after he first entered the room, I knew he was in the wrong grade."

Peter's fifth grade teacher saw him for the first time when he transferred to her small rural school from the large city school where he had completed fourth grade. Born on December 30th in a state which had a December 31st cut-off date, Peter had always been the youngest child in his class.

The teacher's sense that Peter wasn't developmentally ready for fifth grade work was soon confirmed. He didn't understand math concepts; he couldn't follow directions; he needed constant approval. Peter wore a path to the teacher's desk, needing to show her how he'd placed his name on a paper, how he'd put in the margins, how he'd numbered each problem. After three weeks of this, the teacher called his parents.

Peter's parents said school had always been a struggle for their boy, even though he was intelligent. Remedial work had helped him keep moving from grade to grade, but it never helped him reach the point where he could do well without it. When the teacher suggested moving Peter to fourth grade, which would be more appropriate for his current stage of development, his parents agreed at once. Even Peter said, "I'm not ready to be in fifth grade."

That same morning, Peter moved to fourth grade. And, from then on, school work was much easier for him. Gradually, his anxiety about always having to be "right" disappeared.

Heather: The silent sufferer

When Heather was assigned to a third/fourth multi-age classroom, where she was expected to do fourth grade work, she felt overwhelmed. In October, the teacher asked the school's principal to observe Heather. As she sat in her seat and tried to do her math work, tears rolled down her cheeks and onto her paper. The principal asked Heather if she would like to try sliding her desk to the other side of the room and become a third grader for a while. The girl did not wait for an explanation; she made the switch right away.

By simply moving her desk twelve feet, Heather entered a more familiar and comfortable world. She could do third grade work successfully, though she had barely scraped by in school up to that point. Her report card had previously contained a cry for help from someone in an unfair situation. The side which reported academic achievement depicted a poor student; the side which evaluated the person — her work habits, relations with others, ability to take responsibility — described a caring student who tried hard but was unable to succeed in her current grade.

Once Heather had a chance to start over in third grade, success became a possibility, and then a reality. By the time she reached eighth grade, her name appeared regularly on the honor roll.

Joshua: Better late than never

When Joshua Farrington was in eighth grade, his parents, his teacher, and he himself — after much painful soul searching — decided it would be a good idea for him to do eighth grade over again. As Joshua's mother later wrote me, the results made it all worthwhile:

"Another year in eighth grade has made a tremendous difference in Joshua's maturity and readiness for high school. All of his teachers have mentioned the change. I only wish there had been someone there nine years ago to tell us to wait on entering him in school. It could have spared us all so much pain and frustration. Thank you for your part in helping us make this decision."

Joshua summed up his feelings about his experience in the following poem:

I am glad I made the choice
To retain and remain,
And not put so much stress on my brain,
For I am a December boy.
- Joshua Farrington, Grade 8, Vermont

CONCLUSION
What Would You Do If It Was Your Child?

It's easy to give advice, isn't it, especially when someone else is responsible for making the final decision. But, when you're the one responsible, and the decision will have a tremendous impact — for better or worse — on the life of a young child you care deeply about, the stakes are much higher.

Sometimes, of course, the decision can still be an easy one. When a child clearly needs more time to grow, the parents are supportive, and the school offers appropriate extra-time options, the whole decision-making process is relatively easy, which is exactly how it should be. Unfortunately, in many cases the child's situation is more ambiguous, the parents are reluctant or divided, and the school system is failing to provide an extra-time option that meets the child's needs.

More than a few parents and educators who have found themselves in this sort of situation will read my books or listen to what I have to say, and then ask, "It all sounds good, Jim, but what would you do if it was your child who was developmentally young?"

My answer is that one reason I believe so strongly in giving children the time to grow and succeed is that my own child, Caleb, started first grade when he was almost 7-years-old. He experienced the benefits of having extra time firsthand, and my wife and I are convinced that his older age provided him with a "safety net" — we found that he could cope with all of school's demands, while some of the early starters in his grade had a much more difficult time.

When Caleb was in second grade, a "phantom virus" resulted in his staying home from school for five weeks, but he came through the school year with flying colors anyhow. Being older than the average second grader, he had the maturity needed to survive a long-term absence. But, had Caleb started first grade a year sooner, I am sure a lengthy absence would have caused him to fail.

When developmentally young children are placed in a grade or program for which they are not ready, they should receive an ironclad guarantee that during their education they will never have a marginal teacher, never suffer from a long-term illness or injury, and never experience such serious adversity as a parental divorce or the death of a close family member. But, as we all know, in real life there are no such guarantees, and that is why I would not want to take such a chance with my own child's future.

I can also say that as I have advised parents about these difficult issues during the last few decades, I have heard the same refrain over and over again, after an older child has been reassigned to the right grade: "If only we had known, we would have given him the extra time much sooner."

Myth vs. Reality

Just as deciding that a child needs extra time can be difficult, overcoming other adults' resistance to this approach can also prove challenging. As noted elsewhere in this book, some schools are reluctant to provide extra-time options, despite compelling research which shows that many children benefit from such programs. These days, friends, neighbors, family members, and other educators may also have strong beliefs about the pros and cons of extra-time options. So, parents and educators who want to let children have the time they need to develop should be prepared to encounter and overcome the concerns and objections of others.

The Question and Answer Section in the Appendix of this book provides more detailed information about a number of important issues, but some of the myths about extra time deserve to be quickly debunked right here and now.

myth (mith) *noun* An unverifiable belief; an unfounded or false notion.

Myth: Research shows that extra-time options do not provide benefits.
Reality: This myth is primarily based on studies by Laurie Shepard and Mary Lee Smith, which have since been shown to be seriously flawed. As documented in the book, *School Readiness and Transition Programs: Real Facts from Real Schools*, by James Uphoff, Ed.D., these studies inaccurately reported other research, ignored important social and emotional benefits, and are based on unreliable standardized achievement test scores. Dr. Uphoff's book and other studies document numerous extra-time options which have worked successfully in American schools for many years.

Myth: A "developmentally appropriate" curriculum eliminates the need for extra-time options.
Reality: Time and curriculum are two totally different issues, and no curriculum eliminates the need for children to grow and learn at their own rate. Proponents of this myth have failed for years to identify a single school anywhere in the U.S. where the curriculum allows every student to proceed successfully through all the grades without ever needing extra time. Parents and educators should therefore suspect and challenge any "expert" who wants to remove the concept of time-flexibility from developmentally appropriate education.

Myth: Individualized remedial instruction eliminates the need for extra-time options.
Reality: Remedial instruction is a great help to students, but it does not automatically enable every student to succeed in school. Many developmentally young students who receive remedial instruction still need extra time in order to proceed successfully through school. And, remedial instruction not only

takes time away from other activities, it is a reactive intervention used once a student is already struggling and developing negative attitudes, rather than a proactive, early intervention that allows children to succeed and develop positive attitudes right from the start.

Myth: Extra-time options are unnecessary, because all children will catch up by third grade.

Reality: As noted elsewhere in this book, this myth defies common sense as well as the realities experienced in schools across America. The underlying premise for this myth is a theory of development which states that by about age 9, all children reach the developmental stage at which they *are capable* of performing certain types of work. Obviously, however, four years of unsuccessful learning experiences are not simply or suddenly overcome just because a child reaches a new stage of development. An overplaced 9-year-old with insufficient knowledge and a negative attitude remains at a severe disadvantage compared to classmates who have far more knowledge and confidence.

Myth: Extra-time options stigmatize students and damage their self-esteem.

Reality: People stigmatize other people and damage their self-esteem. This is most likely to happen to students when they struggle in school and fail to master the curriculum, whether they are socially promoted to the next grade or not. Most extra-time options are proactive, early interventions designed to prevent children from failing, so the children can avoid the stigma and damaged self-esteem which too often occur when students are not ready for a particular grade or program.

Myth: Any extra-time option is retention.

Reality: Anyone with a clear understanding of the English language and American schools knows that retention means spending another year in the same grade. Extra-time options such as continuous-progress readiness and transition programs allow children to move on to a new grade with a different curriculum and a different teacher. These sorts of programs are positive, proactive alternatives to retention, and someone unable or unwilling to recognize the differences is denying reality.

Myth: Extra-time options are too expensive.
Reality: The availability of extra-time options can reduce the number of children who are identified as needing remedial instruction or special education services, which are not only expensive but often ineffective for developmentally young children. Deliberately failing to teach students effectively can initially decrease an education budget, but the total cost of this policy to a taxpayer is likely to be far higher in the long term, when the cost of increased social services, new prisons, and decreased economic competitiveness are also figured in.

What if there are no viable options?

Amazingly enough, some parents of developmentally young, primary grade children may gather the information they need, do the best they can on their children's behalf, but still find that continuous-progress, extra-time options are unavailable, and that spending an extra year in the same grade is prohibited. What happens then?

One possibility, of course, is to send the child to a private school. Not so surprisingly, many fine private schools encourage a number of their entering students to repeat a grade when transferring from another school — even at the high school level. These "prep" schools, which send many of their students on to prestigious colleges, have achieved their success by providing many students with the extra time needed to master the curriculum, rather than basing the students' grade placement solely on "wax volume certification" — the number of candles on a birthday cake.

Private schools, however, can be very expensive, and in this day and age it is entirely possible that an informed, caring parent may simply have to allow a developmentally young child to be socially promoted from grade to grade through a public school system — always struggling, frequently failing, growing more negative, and never attaining the knowledge and success to which the child is entitled.

In this sort of situation, providing ongoing emotional support for the child is just as important as any particular program, plan, contract, or other half-measure. A child like this is being made to suffer the consequences of the school system's failure, and the child's saying "I hate school" is an entirely natural and understandable response. Working with and supporting the child — while joining with other parents and educators to put unrelenting pressure on the (in)appropriate administrators — is the adults' responsibility.

It would be nice to think that someday the federal, state, and local governments will join together to prevent any children from suffering in this way, but I believe it is very unlikely that the needed changes will come from the top down. I think it is far more likely — and even more desirable — for change to come from the bottom up. Change generated from the "grass roots," rather than government-mandated change, tends to be based on the firsthand experience, which is what is needed for a reform to solve the problem and have lasting power.

We now have the understanding and capabilities to provide supportive educational experiences for our children. Accepting the children as they are — not as we wish them to be — will save a great many of them from failing and hating school.

APPENDIX A

Answers To Questions Parents Frequently Ask About Developmental Readiness & Extra-Time Options

How can a parent know if a child needs an extra year before entering a grade or program?

Parents generally have good instincts regarding their children's needs, and parents who think a child might need extra time can take a number of steps that will help them arrive at the right decision. Let me illustrate this point by telling you about one particular mother, who was concerned about her son.

She had noticed that the boy was shy and quiet in social situations which involved several children, though he was comfortable when just with a few other children. This mother obtained and read information on developmental readiness, including the Signs and Signals of School Stress (see Chapter 4); she talked with teachers at the local school about the curriculum and their experiences with other children; and she shared her concerns with her husband. They considered information about their child's preschool experiences, as well as the results of a developmental assessment, and then decided together to give their son an extra year in kindergarten. It's a decision they've never regretted.

If you have concerns about your child's readiness, I would suggest following this mother's lead: trust your instincts, obtain advice from educators, read the literature (you'll find the names of some excellent publications in the bibliography of this book), and have your child take a developmental assessment. Then, discuss the situation thoroughly with your spouse, so that you can arrive at a joint decision. If you follow these suggestions, I'm confident that your decision will be the right one for your child.

Aren't there things I can do at home to increase my child's readiness?

Providing a healthy and supportive home environment for your child is extremely important, but it will not change the rate at which your child develops. And, too much pressure or early "academic training" can actually make it more difficult for your child to succeed in school.

Some steps that help prepare a child for school include reading stories aloud every day, limiting the type and amount of television watched, and making sure the child receives proper nutrition and rest. In addition, young children should have plenty of time to "play" with water, sand, clay, and other materials, all of which actually teach children important lessons about their world and themselves. A child who has a background filled with these sorts of experiences may still be a "late bloomer," however, and need extra time to develop in order to succeed in school.

While providing guidance and appropriate experiences, parents must be sensitive to their child's interests and current stage of development. If a preschooler is not yet interested in learning to read, efforts to "make" the young child learn to read may lead to negative attitudes and feelings of incompetence, as well as learning problems that will interfere with the child's education in later years. Focusing on what a young child is ready to learn helps the child more than efforts to make the child "measure up" — before and after the child starts school.

If you have ever forced a bud to open before it was ready to bloom, you know that premature exposure leads to failure. What could have been a beautiful and long-lived flower soon withers and dies from being pushed ahead of nature's wise timing and design. Children unfold and bloom when they are ready, just as flowers do. We cannot speed up the process, nor should we want to interfere with this vital aspect of a young child's life.

Doesn't kindergarten make kids ready for first grade?

Kindergarten cannot "force-feed" readiness or "make" children develop at a faster rate. And, in order to succeed in many first grade programs, children must be able to meet certain standards, particularly in regard to reading and writing, which then become the basis for the following year's work. A child who needs more time to develop is unlikely to succeed in this sort of program, no matter how much preparation a kindergarten provides.

Kindergarten does many wonderful things for children. It provides stimulating, creative activities that interest children and help them build healthy bodies and minds. It is a key transitional experience between home and school that provides important opportunities for children to learn together. A high-quality kindergarten program supports all four aspects of children's development — emotional, social, physical, and intellectual — but it cannot and should not push children beyond their biological limits. Rather than attempting the impossible task of making every child ready for first grade in one year, schools can and should provide extra-time options that allow children to continue growing and learning at different rates throughout the primary grades.

Isn't is really only the "slow" kids who need more time to develop?

Some of the very brightest children need extra time in order to succeed in school. This is particularly true of "late bloomers," who may be highly intelligent but have not yet reached the developmental stage at which they are ready for a particular grade or program. Their current rate of development may be slower than that of many of their chronological peers, but they may in fact be able to perform intellectual or other tasks faster than these same peers. And, once they are correctly placed in the right grade or program, there is nothing slow about the progress these children make in school.

Even when children seem to be "early bloomers" who are intellectually ready for a particular grade or program, they may still benefit from having extra time to develop. For some bright children, the easiest part of school is the academic work, but academic achievement does not necessarily equal success in school. When a child always has his or her "head in a book," with insufficient time and energy left over for social, emotional, and physical development, the child may not be happy. And, this sort of lop-sided development may lead to problems that undermine the child's academic success in later years.

Kindergarten teachers are often pressured to advance intelligent children into first grade, regardless of their overall pattern of development. Teachers who resist this sort of pressure deserve praise and support, because they are taking steps to help a child succeed in all the important areas of development, including the intellectual realm.

Aren't children who participate in extra-time options embarrassed to be older and bigger than their classmates, especially when they move into the later elementary grades?

Some children may experience momentary feelings of embarrassment because of their size and age, but this is far preferable to enduring the years of daily humiliation and shame that occur when children feel stupid and are unable to do the same work that many classmates complete easily. This is especially true in the later elementary grades, when the lack of knowledge and negative attitudes that result from overplacement may cause serious problems at home and at school.

In many cases, children who are physically larger and older than their classmates become leaders and are "looked up to" by others in the same grade or program. Their muscle coordination and physical abilities often surpass those of their peers, and they have the confidence and maturity that encourage respect and friendship.

If a child can "keep up" by using remedial services, isn't that better than having to repeat a grade?

Consider Matt, whom you read about in Chapter 3. He was so busy with remedial work that he did not have sufficient time for play, which is an important part of the learning process for young children. And, Matt began to develop negative attitudes about school and himself, because he could not truly succeed in school even with the extra help. It was only when Matt took extra time and was placed in the proper grade that he no longer needed special services and began to enjoy school.

Children who cannot succeed in school by themselves often learn to hate school and themselves. In too many cases, an effort is being made to help the children do work they are not developmentally ready for, so much of the effort goes to waste. And, children who were already feeling "dumb" because they could not do the work feel even "dumber" when so much extra effort does not seem to help.

Remedial services can and do help many children, but placement in the correct grade or program is usually the best solution for all concerned.

What's wrong with putting pressure on a child to measure up? Isn't challenge an important part of growth?

Challenge is an important part of growth, but these days school is challenging enough without deliberately putting a young child at an unfair disadvantage.

Any pressure or challenge for a young child should be appropriate in regard to both its purpose and intensity. Just as it would be foolish and even cruel to pressure a child to grow taller, you cannot pressure a young child to develop faster. A stimulating and supportive environment will support the child's development, but the rate and stage of a child's development is largely determined by physiological processes such as brain maturation, which the child does not and cannot control. A child who is pressured to do the impossible is likely to develop emotional problems and negative attitudes which interfere with learning.

Even when adults apply pressure on a child to do something which is possible, this approach can backfire. Some children deliberately rebel because their wishes are ignored too often and they feel they are being treated unfairly. Other children become overly acquiescent and fail to develop the independence and self-esteem which contribute to success and happiness in later life. Still other children respond well initially but "burn out" a few years later, losing interest just when their enthusiasm and involvement with school-related activities should be increasing.

Older children tend to handle pressure and challenge better, especially if they have already developed a strong sense of confidence and self-esteem. This is far more likely to occur when adult caregivers recognize that early childhood should be a precious — not a pressured — time.

Don't educators recommend "social promotion" when a child moves beyond the primary grades?

Most school officials avoid using the term "social promotion," even though that is exactly what some do encourage.

Social promotion is the automatic promotion of all children from one grade to the next, regardless of the children's academic and developmental progress. While this policy is supposed to protect children from feeling badly about themselves, it often achieves the opposite effect. It does, however, protect some school officials from difficult decisions, confrontations with parents, and budgetary pressures.

Instead of protecting children, social promotion often keeps children feeling helpless and inadequate, as they continue to struggle through programs in which they cannot truly succeed. At the same time, social promotion also prevents children from acquiring the knowledge which they can and should obtain as part of their education.

Some school officials, meanwhile, find that social promotion helps them avoid the extra costs involved in having children spend more time in school. (The costs of special education services often skyrocket simultaneously, but this may come out of someone else's budget.) By lowering a school's standards to the point at which chronological age is the only standard, social promotion allows every single student to become a high school graduate in exactly thirteen years. Whether these high school graduates can read and write or add and subtract simply does not matter.

Fortunately, most school officials recognize that this is a cruel, destructive cop-out. While some ideological extremists and ivory-tower theorists still want to prohibit any form of extra time, the existence of true academic standards in the upper grades means that some children will continue to need extra time in order to make real progress through those grades. If parents and educators want to avoid having to make an "either or" choice between upper-grade retention and social promotion, there must be extra-time options in the early primary grades.

If some educators oppose providing extra time while others favor it, who should I believe?

At one of the talks I gave to a parent group, one father told of his struggle to make the right decision about his son's placement in school. Let me share with you what he said, since his story is very similar to what many other parents have told me, and it contains what I think is the best advice on the subject.

"When someone first suggested that we give our son an extra year," the father explained, "my reaction was negative.

"My wife and I talked to a lot of people about developmental readiness, including many teachers. A number of people involved with education gave us advice, and much of it was contradictory — we kept getting mixed messages.

"Finally, we talked to several parents who had given their child an extra year, and to several parents who had not. What we heard from them became our bottom line:

"We found that a lot of parents who did *not* give their child an extra year wished they had, but we never found a single mother or father who had given a child an extra year and then regretted it.

"We gave our son an additional year of preschool, and we are very, very happy with the result."

APPENDIX B

Letters From A Parent Concerned About Her Child

November 14, 1993

Dear Mr. Grant,

My son started kindergarten in August of 1990 when he was 5-years-old. His birthday is in June. He was always very bright and quick to learn things, so I figured he could go ahead and start school at the age of 5.

At first, he didn't have any problems other than crying occasionally over little things. In first grade, he started out okay but grew increasingly frustrated over his work and seemed to struggle with reading and writing. He did wonderfully in math, though. We were told we could retain him if we wanted to, but I thought that would really kill his self-esteem, of which he had little.

We sent him on to second grade and everything just got worse. He was frustrated when writing. He had trouble keeping up with the teacher. He had a little trouble with reading but still loved math. He was smaller in size than the other kids and that bothered him. He would throw occasional tantrums and was basically ignored when he did this. This was my fault because I work at the school as an aide, and I knew his teachers and would tell them to be gentle with him, because I thought we were trying to help his self-esteem.

Eventually, we were told that maybe we should take him to a psychologist to have him tested for Learning Disability problems or a possible Attention Deficit Disorder. We decided to go ahead and do that, and after 5 sessions the therapist could not pinpoint any L.D. or A.D.D., but she did suggest that we put him on a medication such as Prozac. I absolutely did not want to this unless I had specific information that he had a real problem. His behaviors were crying easily, certain clothing that bothered him, and easy frustration. We stopped going to the therapist, because during the summer he did so much better and seemed to mature more.

We did hold him back for another year in second grade, though. His teacher strongly recommended this, and she was such a wonderful teacher that we thought he would be fine. The first week was okay, but then he started getting angry and throwing little fits in class. My husband and I were called to the principal's office one morning because of this (I know her well because I work there), and she said we must do something about this behavior. After discussing options, we decided a "get-tough" approach might help. We called our son into the office and told him we were no longer going to put up with this kind of behavior, and the principal would come to get him if he ever acted like this again.

After that meeting and a long talk with our son, he has improved 100%. That was two months ago, and I cannot believe the difference in his whole attitude. I think he feels so much better about himself, and he feels much more comfortable with this class. He has a new confidence, and his writing and art work are much improved. He even narrated a class play, which is something he would never have done before.

After reading your book, I now know that he was just in the wrong class for his age, and another factor was a lack of "follow-through" discipline. He was spoiled and used to getting his way, and I think that added to the problem. But, while I did not really favor retention, I am definitely in favor of it now for young or emotionally young kids.

Your book has been in circulation with several teachers at our school, and I think everyone is seeing it positively. Thank you for your work.

May 17, 1994

Dear Mr. Grant,

Just to let you know, our son's ISTEP test scores have now come back, and he scored far above the national average in all skills and excelled on the mathematics portion of the test. There are still a few things on which we have to work with him, but he is so much improved. I am anxious to see how well he does next year in third grade with a teacher of a different style and attitude.

Thank you for reading my letters.

(Name & address withheld at the writer's request.)

Bibliography

Ames, Louise Bates. *Raising Good Kids*. Rosemont, NJ: Modern Learning Press/Programs For Education, 1992.

Ames, Louise Bates. *What Am I Doing In This Grade?* Rosemont, NJ: Modern Learning Press/Programs For Education, 1985.

Arent, Ruth P. *Stress and Your Child*. Englewood Cliffs, NJ: Prentice-Hall, 1984.

Boyer, Ernest. *Ready to Learn*. Princeton, NJ: Carnegie Foundation for the Advancement of Teaching.

Brazelton, T. Berry. *Touchpoints*. New York, NY: Addison-Wesley, 1992.

Buros, Jay. *Why Whole Language?* Rosemont, NJ: Modern Learning Press/Programs For Education, 1991.

Carll, Barbara and Nancy Richard. *One Piece of the Puzzle*. Rosemont, NJ: Modern Learning Press/Programs For Education, 1970.

Cohen, Miriam. *First Grade Takes A Test*. New York: Dell Publishing, 1983.

Coletta, Anthony. *What's Best For Kids*. Rosemont, NJ: Modern Learning Press/Programs For Education, 1991.

Coplan, Theresa and Frank. *The Early Childhood Years*. New York: Putnam Publishing, 1983.

Elkind, David. *The Hurried Child*. Reading, MA: Addison-Wesley, 1981.

Elkind, David. *Miseducation*. New York: Alfred Knopf, 1988.

George, Paul. *How to Untrack Your School.* Alexandria, VA: Association for Supervision and Curriculum Development, 1992.

Goodman, Gretchen. *Inclusive Classrooms from A to Z: A Handbook for Teachers.* Columbus, OH: Teacher's Publishing Group: 1994.

Grant, Jim. *Developmental Education in the 1990's.* Rosemont, NJ: Programs For Education/Modern Learning Press, 1992.

Grant, Jim. *Worth Repeating.* Rosemont, NJ: Programs For Education/Modern Learning Press, 1989.

Grant, Jim and Johnson, Bob. *A Common Sense Guide to Multiage Practices.* Columbus, OH: Teachers' Publishing Group, 1994.

Greene, Lawrence J. *Kids Who Underachieve.* New York: Basic Books, 1985.

Healy, Jane. *Endangered Minds.* New York: Simon & Schuster, 1990.

Hobby, Janice Hale. *Staying Back.* Gainesville, FL: Triad Publishing Company, 1990.

Keshner, Judy. *Starting School.* Rosemont, NJ: Modern Learning Press, 1992.

Kraus, Robert. *Leo the Late Bloomer.* New York: Windmill Books, 1981.

Moore, Sheila and Roon Frost. *The Little Boy, A Guide to the First Eight Years.* New York: Clarkson N. Potter, 1986.

National Association of Elementary School Principals. *Early Childhood Education and the Elementary School Principal.* Alexandria, VA.

Osman, Betty B. *No One To Play With*. New York: Warner Books, 1982.

Uphoff, James. *School Readiness and Transition Programs: Real Facts from Real Schools*. Rosemont, NJ: Modern Learning Press/Programs For Education, 1991.

Uphoff, James. *Summer Children*. ?, OH: J&J Publishing, 1986.

Vail, Priscilla. *About Dyslexia*. Rosemont, NJ: Modern Learning Press/Programs For Education, 1990.

Vail, Priscilla. *Common Ground: Whole Language and Phonics Working Together*. Rosemont, NJ: Modern Learning Press/Programs For Education, 1991.

Vail, Priscilla. *Emotion: The On/Off Switch For Learning*. Rosemont, NJ: Modern Learning Press/Programs For Education, 1994.

Vail, Priscilla. *Learning Styles*. Rosemont, NJ: Modern Learning Press/Programs For Education, 1992.

Winn, Marie. *Children Without Childhood*. New York: Penguin Books, 1983.

Index

Other Publications by Jim Grant
Available from
Modern Learning Press/Programs for Education

Jim Grant's Book of Parent Pages

*Every Parent's Owner's Manuals
for 3, 4, 5, 6 & 7 year-olds*

Do You Know Where Your Child Is? (video)

Worth Repeating

Worth Repeating (video)

Childhood Should Be A Precious Time

Developmental Education In The 1990's

call toll-free
1-800-627-5867

Or write
Modern Learning Press/Programs for Education
P.O. Box 167
Rosemont, NJ 08556

Quarter Past September

Grant

When it's quarter past September
It's a magic time of life.

The school world of our children
Should be free of strife.

Our little people have waited and waited...
And waited for this day, only to
Learn that school is not
A place for play.

The teacher welcomes one and all
And asks them to sit still,
Most of the children are quick to comply,
Except for overplaced Bill.

The children were given their phonics
Lesson and asked to complete the job,
Everyone finished all their work,
Except for overplaced Bob.

The painters were careful with
The paint—the teachers said "don't spill."
And all the painters got the message,
Except for overplaced Jill.

At recess time a reminder
Came not to run and race:
No one forgot this simple rule,
Except for overplaced Grace.

At the Halloween party, the
Teacher cautioned, "please don't
Spill your juice," everyone was
Careful, except overplaced Bruce.

They love their big new pencils,
They love the color red.
Everyone knows the correct way to hold it
Except for overplaced Ed.

The list of children overplaced is
All a too familiar case.

Shouldn't we watch for signals
And signs that children give
Off that they need extra time.

Parent pressure—state law, too,
Send us youngsters before they're due.

High content curriculum we must abide,
But children keep falling by the wayside.

One hundred years from today,
What difference does age make, we'll say.

St. Peter won't stop you at the pearly gate
To ask your age when you graduate.

So many children in their prime
Desperately need the gift of time.

Let's make school a place to succeed
And give our children the time they need.

Published by
Modern Learning Press
Rosemont, New Jersey 08556
© 1986 C. James Grant
Item #197

help

SALE